THE GROWTH OF PUBLIC EMPLOYMENT

IN GREAT BRITAIN

NATIONAL BUREAU OF ECONOMIC RESEARCH

NUMBER 60, GENERAL SERIES

The Growth
of Public Employment
in Great Britain

MOSES ABRAMOVITZ
STANFORD UNIVERSITY

VERA F. ELIASBERG
NATIONAL BUREAU OF ECONOMIC RESEARCH

A STUDY BY THE
NATIONAL BUREAU OF ECONOMIC RESEARCH, NEW YORK

PUBLISHED BY
PRINCETON UNIVERSITY PRESS, PRINCETON
1957

Printed in the United States of America
by Princeton University Press, Princeton, New Jersey

Relation of the Directors
to the Work and Publications
of the National Bureau of Economic Research

1. The object of the National Bureau of Economic Research is to ascertain and to present to the public important economic facts and their interpretation in a scientific and impartial manner. The Board of Directors is charged with the responsibility of ensuring that the work of the National Bureau is carried on in strict conformity with this object.

2. To this end the Board of Directors shall appoint one or more Directors of Research.

3. The Director or Directors of Research shall submit to the members of the Board, or to its Executive Committee, for their formal adoption, all specific proposals concerning researches to be instituted.

4. No report shall be published until the Director or Directors of Research shall have submitted to the Board a summary drawing attention to the character of the data and their utilization in the report, the nature and treatment of the problems involved, the main conclusions and such other information as in their opinion would serve to determine the suitability of the report for publication in accordance with the principles of the National Bureau.

5. A copy of any manuscript proposed for publication shall also be submitted to each member of the Board. For each manuscript to be so submitted a special committee shall be appointed by the President, or at his designation by the Executive Director, consisting of three Directors selected as nearly as may be one from each general division of the Board. The names of the special manuscript committee shall be stated to each Director when the summary and report described in paragraph (4) are sent to him. It shall be the duty of each member of the committee to read the manuscript. If each member of the special committee signifies his approval within thirty days, the manuscript may be published. If each member of the special committee has not signified his approval within thirty days of the transmittal of the report and manuscript, the Director of Research shall then notify each member of the Board, requesting approval or disapproval of publication, and thirty additional days shall be granted for this purpose. The manuscript shall then not be published unless at least a majority of the entire Board and a two-thirds majority of those members of the Board who shall have voted on the proposal within the time fixed for the receipt of votes on the publication proposed shall have approved.

6. No manuscript may be published, though approved by each member of the special committee, until forty-five days have elapsed from the transmittal of the summary and report. The interval is allowed for the receipt of any memorandum of dissent or reservation, together with a brief statement of his reasons, that any member may wish to express; and such memorandum of dissent or reservation shall be published with the manuscript if he so desires. Publication does not, however, imply that each member of the Board has read the manuscript, or that either members of the Board in general, or of the special committee, have passed upon its validity in every detail.

7. A copy of this resolution shall, unless otherwise determined by the Board, be printed in each copy of every National Bureau book.

(Resolution adopted October 25, 1926 and revised February 6, 1933 and February 24, 1941)

PREFACE

WORK on this study began in September 1951. A brief preliminary report of its results was made in a paper presented to the American Economic Association in December 1952. The first draft of the full report was completed at the same time, and this explains the fact that, in general, our review of the trend of government employment in Great Britain stops with 1950. Successive revisions and other work have prevented publication until the present time. Although some important changes in the size of British government staffs, particularly of the central government staff, have occurred since 1950, they have hardly altered the character of the long-term trends which it is the main purpose of the book to describe. Some of the more striking developments since 1950 in the size and functions of the central government staff are described in Chapter 4.

Investigators who study the history of a foreign country are especially dependent on the help of knowledgeable critics. Our study was read by Solomon Fabricant, Daniel M. Holland, M. Slade Kendrick, and George Stigler, of the research staff of the National Bureau of Economic Research, and by three of the Bureau's directors, E. Wight Bakke, H. W. Laidler, and Clarence Heer. We are grateful to all these reviewers for useful suggestions.

The manuscript was also read by Professor Harold Barger of Columbia University, Professor Samuel J. Hurwitz of Brooklyn College, and Mr. Alan T. Peacock of the London School of Economics and Political Science. We are particularly indebted to these readers whose more intimate knowledge of Britain and of the recent history of the British government and its social policy enabled us to eliminate many errors and to sustain a certain confidence in the general reliability of our treatment. Needless to say, none of our readers are in any way responsible for the failings that may still mark our work.

We should also like to record a serious debt to the staff of the British Information Services in New York. Their advice, patiently and freely given, widened our knowledge of sources and warned us of pitfalls in their use. The files and shelves of their library held a rich and convenient collection of data.

The manuscript benefited from the editorial advice of Ellen V. Seiler. Our charts were prepared by H. Irving Forman.

Moses Abramovitz
Vera F. Eliasberg

July 10, 1956

CONTENTS

CONTENTS

TABLES

CHARTS

xiii

xii

THE GROWTH OF PUBLIC EMPLOYMENT

IN GREAT BRITAIN

CHAPTER 1

THE MEASURE OF GOVERNMENT

DURING the last half century, governments nearly everywhere have become more powerful influences in economic life. As yet, however, little is known in quantitative terms about the size governments have attained, the rapidity of their growth, what functions they have assumed, how large these functions loom, and what differences can be observed among countries. This study is part of a larger investigation by the National Bureau of Economic Research, the general aim of which is to provide answers to these questions.[1] The purpose of the present study is more limited. It is based upon only one measure of the size of government, namely, the number of persons directly employed by government agencies, and it is for the most part concerned with but one country, Great Britain.[2] The information on employment is traced for a sixty-year period, from 1890 to 1950, in as systematic a fashion as we could manage, but we also include a less systematic survey of developments in the nineteenth century and a brief comparison of the broad features of the British experience with those of the United States.[3]

The ingredients of our study are of three broad kinds. First, there are the statistics of public employment in Great Britain, the compilation of which was the primary objective of the investigation. These are presented in the context of a brief account of economic and political changes and of the development of ideas and attitudes in Britain which we hope may help to illuminate the statistical record. This account may be taken to be the second ingredient. Finally, we have tried at convenient places to suggest

[1] An earlier publication has dealt with the United States (see Solomon Fabricant, *The Trend of Government Activity in the United States since 1900*, National Bureau of Economic Research, 1952). Alan T. Peacock of the London School of Economics and Political Science is now conducting a study of British government expenditures.

[2] By Great Britain we mean England, Wales, and Scotland, and so far as possible our data refer to those three rather than to the United Kingdom, including Ireland.

[3] The writers have made an earlier report of their work. See "The Trend of Public Employment in Great Britain and the United States," *American Economic Review, Papers and Proceedings*, May 1953, pp. 203-215. This was a summary of the investigation at an early stage. The present report is based on much additional work and reflects revisions in the underlying data.

certain hypotheses concerning the causes of the growth of public employment, which would otherwise be implicit in our work.

It is almost needless to point out that, in a book as short as this, the historical account we provide as a background for the statistical measures is necessarily far from complete. But we have tried to touch on the more important matters. Similarly, the causal hypotheses we entertain, whatever their plausibility, are not as yet well tested. On that account, they might have been permitted to remain unexpressed. Since some theoretical speculation, however, guides all historical accounts and even the selection and arrangement of statistics, we have thought it more candid and perhaps more interesting to state our tentative hypotheses. Whatever their value as guides to further research, however, these ideas still must be confronted with a much wider range of experience and, no doubt, be more or less extensively modified before they emerge as well-founded generalizations.

To appreciate the relevance of employment measures to the more general question of the role of government in economic life, we should recognize that the relation of the state to the economy has two aspects. First of all, governments act as economic agents. That is to say, they participate directly in the activities of the economy. They buy goods, hire labor and other productive factors, and organize them for the output of goods and services. Some of this output is sold, some given away, and much of it applied to public purposes of a more diffuse or intangible sort. The state's agencies raise revenue, borrow and lend, save and invest. Their operations are part of a nation's total production and part of its mechanism for the distribution of money income and of real goods and services. Through actual participation, therefore, states influence the operation of all productive processes and the working of all markets. In all these ways states are economic agents coordinate with other primary economic agents, such as individuals, households, and business firms and other private associations.

The second aspect of government in its relation to economic life is its more obvious influence as a regulator, that is, as a political agent. By fundamental law, by statute, by administrative order, and by judicial decree the state regulates to a greater or lesser degree the actions of the various economic agents, including the actions of its own agencies.

These two aspects are connected. Since regulation involves the services of men and the raising and expenditure of income, the state becomes an economic agent if only with regard to the resources and revenues it needs to function as a political agent. And insofar as the state participates in economic life in order to produce goods and services of various sorts, it inevitably exerts an influence on every market in which it acts. As the importance of this fact becomes more widely appreciated, governments tend to plan even their productive operations with a view to influencing private economic activity. For example, investment in government enterprises in both Great Britain and the United States is, to some extent, pushed forward or held back in order to help stabilize the community's income and employment.

As between these two aspects in which the state appears in relation to the economy, this study is only indirectly relevant to the government's role as a political agent. True, we measure the number of persons engaged in regulatory functions, but we have no way of gauging the influence of their work. The study is more directly concerned with the question: How large have British governments grown in the performance of the various functions in which they participate? But even to this question we can give only a qualified reply. The nature of the restrictions upon the significance of our data becomes apparent if we consider some of the measures which are relevant with respect to the importance of government as economic agent.

If we want to know the value of the resources which the state causes to be devoted to its own purposes, we must measure the total expenditures of all governments in that country, after deducting transfer payments. Such a comprehensive measure would take into account not only the resources employed directly by agencies of the state but also those employed by private contractors—and their subcontractors—in supplying goods or services purchased by the state. Employment of labor by government agencies may be some indicator of this total, in the same way that aggregate employment is sometimes used as an index of the national income. It would be a faulty index, however, for not only may there be changes in the ratio of labor to other resources employed in the production of goods for government, but there may also be changes in the ratio of goods directly produced by government agencies to goods purchased.

We may also be interested in knowing how large a share of all resources is directly used in the work of government agencies as compared with the share used by private producers. A complete answer would require information not only about the labor employed, but also about the capital and land used. Labor employment data used alone are presumably better indicators of the direct absorption of resources by government than of total absorption, but they will still be at fault to the extent that there are changes in the ratio of labor to other resources employed. Differences in this ratio will also throw doubt on the usefulness of labor data as an indicator of the value of all resources employed directly by governments when we use them in international comparisons or in comparisons among different functions.

These limitations on the significance of our data are serious. We can only warn the reader about them and urge him to await the appearance of supplementary information.[4]

Measures of labor employment by governments, however, have substantial intrinsic interest. Governments are peculiar employers with their own characteristic criteria for employment and advancement. They offer special conditions of work, of discipline and reward, and they bring to the labor market an element of demand whose structure and pattern of change are different from those presented by the private sector. As employers, governments are subject to the peculiar influences of politics. Their operations are exempt from the test of money profit, but they must normally operate within the rigid pecuniary framework set by legislative appropriations. Their workers' status and advancement are commonly guarded by legislation and administrative decree, but they are also threatened by the pressure of party and personal favor. For many of their workers, in some cases for the bulk of them, governments offer secure careers through established grades to pensioned retirement. But many officials also face the danger of arbitrary discharge or unmerited neglect for causes unique to public service. Government work, therefore, provides its own characteristic blend of security and risk.

The special functions of governments make the sex, occupational, and educational compositions of their staffs different from those of private industry. Moreover, since government output has its own special trend, this is imparted to the demand for the kinds of workers governments wish to hire. And since the bulk of government output is financed by taxes rather than by sales

[4] See the reference above to the study by Alan T. Peacock (note 1).

revenue, government demand for labor responds to business cycles in ways peculiarly its own.

It is clearly desirable that the many special characteristics of governments as employers should, as soon as possible, be described with the accuracy and detail they deserve. Meanwhile we can be confident of the existence of pervasive differences between government and private employment and between the influence of governments and those of private employers on the labor market. It is, therefore, well to know how large a segment of the labor force is now working for governments compared with former years and why the segment has grown so rapidly.

The order of our argument is, briefly, as follows: In the next chapter we survey the major developments in the growth of the British government in the nineteenth century. Although quantitative information is scant, the survey furnishes an extended background which helps to clarify the period since 1890, for which we have prepared a statistical record. The third chapter presents a general view of the expansion of government since 1890 in terms of labor employment data. More detailed treatments of the central government, the local authorities, and the nationalized industries follow. The final chapter compares some of the main trends in the size of government in Great Britain with those in the United States.

CHAPTER 2

GOVERNMENT IN NINETEENTH CENTURY GREAT BRITAIN

As THE nineteenth century drew to a close, governments in Great Britain were still small by modern standards. In 1890, only some 3.5 per cent of the labor force consisted of public employees, and the period of rapid expansion in the size of governments was only then opening. Nevertheless, 1890 does not represent the beginning of the great changes which, in the next sixty years, would produce a multifold increase in the share of the labor force used by government. Although our meager evidence suggests that, compared with later developments, no great changes occurred in the 1800's in the size of governments relative to other branches of the economy, significant alterations were made in their structure and functions, alterations which prepared the way for later expansion and which help explain the pace and direction of twentieth century growth.

In the course of the nineteenth century, the British economy assumed its present industrialized and urbanized appearance. By 1890, agriculture and forestry occupied hardly more than 10 per cent of the work force. Some 62 per cent of the people of England and Wales lived in urban areas with a population over 10,000; 40 per cent in areas with a population over 50,000. The mercantilist legislation of earlier centuries had been repealed, but the British people had begun to assign new functions to their governments in order to cope with the problems generated by machine production, capitalist economic organization, and urban life.

"Cobden would hardly recognize the world," wrote the London *Economist* in 1894 in a much-quoted article entitled "The Advance towards State Socialism."[1] Governments had, indeed, begun to multiply their activities and to revise their structure in ways which facilitated later development.

The Adaptation of Government to Industrialization

The response of government to the gradual emergence of industrial capitalism may be traced well back into the eighteenth

[1] Cited in J. H. Clapham, *An Economic History of Modern Britain*, London, Cambridge University Press, 1938, Vol. III, p. 397.

century. So far as this response affected the size of government, its first manifestations were local. The growing urban centers lacked the most elementary facilities to meet their needs for water, drainage, streets, police and fire protection, and certain health measures. These urgent requirements of individual localities were met at first by private bill legislation in Parliament, which usually set up Improvement Commissioners empowered to perform specified duties in newly established Improvement Districts. A very large number of such agencies were established in the latter half of the eighteenth century and the first part of the nineteenth.[2]

The use of *ad hoc* arrangements reflected the pressing needs created by the new conditions, the incapacity of the corrupt and oligarchic municipal corporations, and the equal incapacity of the parish vestries and county justices who constituted such local authority as then existed in rural areas and in newly grown but still unincorporated urban areas. Parliamentary private bills and a multitude of *ad hoc* local authorities were, however, no substitute for a logical structure of local government sufficiently vigorous and powerful to meet local needs and to act as an efficient local agent of the central government.[3]

[2] See Joseph Redlich and F. W. Hirst, *Local Government in England*, London, Macmillan, 1903, Vol. I, p. 131. "Of 708 local Acts which the Municipal Commissioners of 1834 found at work in the boroughs, 400 were passed under George III, 154 under George IV, and 26 under William IV" (*ibid.*, p. 131).

[3] As to the corruption and inefficiency of the local governments of the time, in 1835 the Royal Commission on Municipal Corporations wrote:

"In conclusion, we report to your Majesty that there prevails amongst the inhabitants of a great majority of the incorporated towns a general and, in our opinion, a just dissatisfaction with their municipal institutions, a distrust of the self-elected municipal councils, whose powers are subject to no popular control, and whose acts and proceedings, being secret, are unchecked by the influence of public opinion; a distrust of the municipal magistracy, tainting with suspicion the local administration of justice, and often accompanied with contempt of the persons by whom the law is administered; a discontent under the burthens of local taxation, while revenues that ought to be applied for the public advantage are diverted from their legitimate use and are sometimes wastefully bestowed for the benefit of individuals, sometimes squandered for purposes injurious to the character and morals of the people. We therefore feel it to be our duty to represent to your Majesty that the existing municipal corporations of England and Wales neither possess nor deserve the confidence or respect of your Majesty's subjects, and that a thorough reform must be effected before they can become, what we humbly submit to your Majesty they ought to be, useful

The reforming acts of the 1830's began to meet these needs. The Parliamentary Reform Act of 1832 broadened the franchise and went some distance to adjust the distribution of seats to that of the population. It helped make Parliament a more responsive organ of public opinion, and it also raised the level of local government. For, with the weeding out of rotten boroughs and the extension of the franchise, the opportunity to control Parliamentary seats by corrupting limited local electorates and corporations was reduced and gradually eliminated.

The Poor Law Amendment Act of 1834 combined the minuscule parishes into Poor Law Unions and set Guardians—partly elected, partly appointed—over them. Its emphasis on indoor relief, more rationally organized, was the basis for an uneven, inadequate, but still gradual proliferation of institutions for pauper care—not merely shelters and workhouses, but infirmaries, old age homes, orphanages, and even something like schools. By subjecting the local Guardians to the Central Board of Poor Law Commissioners and its inspectorate, the Act introduced that important device of British government, the local administration of centrally established standards, supervised and inspected by an organ of the national government. For the next fifty years, until the Local Government Acts of 1888 and 1894 set up County Councils and Urban and Rural District Councils, the Poor Law Unions shared with the sanitary authorities an increasing burden of all types of local administration outside the boundaries of the incorporated boroughs.

Finally, the Municipal Corporations Act of 1835 began a fundamental reform of city government. The municipal franchise was extended to the entire body of rate payers, and the municipal council was established as the legal agent of the local community

---

and efficient 'instruments of local government' " (Redlich and Hirst, *op. cit.*, p. 116).

As to the creation of *ad hoc* organs in these circumstances, it is stated that "in most municipal boroughs of any size municipal interests are managed, not by the proper municipal authority, but by special ad hoc bodies (commissioners, local boards, or trustees) constituted under a local Act for such purposes as lighting, drainage, paving, and cleaning the streets and providing the town or a part of it with water. Even the police were generally placed under the management of these new authorities instead of being entrusted to the corporation. . . .

"The divisions of authority not only produced apathy with respect to municipal improvements but also serious discords and riots" (*ibid.*, pp. 120-121).

at large rather than as the personification of a restricted group of corporators. Although the power of the new councils was at first severely limited and even the powers of the old *ad hoc* local authorities were not transferred to them by general act, such transfer was made permissive and gradually accomplished.[4] And as the new municipal governments proved themselves, their sphere of authority was widened by private bill and general legislation. Henceforth they were also treated as the local agents for instituting and administering such measures as were necessary to meet general standards set by Parliament.

Not only the structure but the personnel of government was strengthened in the course of the century. The establishment of the Poor Law Commission inspectorate introduced the expert into British government. The Trevelyan-Northcote investigations (1848-1853) and their impressive report laid the foundation for the modern British civil service. The National Civil Service Commission was established in 1855 as an examining board, but partisan nomination continued for a time. There followed a series of reforms in individual departments until in 1870 the public competitive examination was made the normal entrance to a civil service career. This was followed by improvements in standards of work and promotion.[5] Similar practices were gradually established in local government.

These improvements in the structure and personnel of government were in part adaptations to the needs of the developing industrial economy and to the new functions which government was assuming to meet those needs, in part prerequisites for the later assumption of still larger functions. Of the great array of governmental functions that were assumed and extended in the course of the nineteenth century, two reforms, those of the police and of the Post Office, were outstanding for their effects on the numbers of government employees. The Metropolitan Police Force was established in 1829 and subjected to the control of the Home Secretary. By an Act of 1835, responsibility for police management in the boroughs outside London was uniformly placed upon statutory watch committees of the Town Councils. Finally, in 1856, every county was compelled to employ a paid

[4] By 1879, only 14 out of 240 municipal boroughs possessed a sanitary authority independent of the Town Council (*ibid.*, p. 132).

[5] Hiram Miller Stout, *Public Service in Great Britain*, University of North Carolina Press, 1938, pp. 23-43.

police force, grants-in-aid being made contingent upon the attainment of a standard of efficiency defined by the Home Office and certified by its police inspectors.[6]

The expansion of the Post Office got its great stimulus in 1840 when Rowland Hill, having calculated that the main cost of the postal service was incurred in taxing letters at their starting point and collecting postage on delivery, persuaded the government to disregard distance and introduce a uniform penny post for the United Kingdom.[7] The Post Office was made to serve the Liberal desire to promote education and the interchange of ideas when the book post was started in 1848 and when cheap rates were extended to newspapers in 1870. And it was to serve the Liberal interest in thrift that Gladstone started the Post Office savings banks in 1861.[8]

The success of uniform penny post helped persuade the government in 1868 to absorb the telegraph system into the Post Office. Private companies had developed the telegraph in Britain, but many localities found themselves without service and, for a time, fees and services varied from district to district. In spite of the prevailing sentiment against state enterprise, the Associated Chambers of Commerce petitioned for government ownership and Parliament was induced to buy out the existing firms.[9]

Other governmental initiatives were less demanding of manpower but highly significant in opening up a broad range of activities and in causing a slow accretion to the size of the state. In 1833 the first Factory Act equipped with an enforcement mechanism was passed. It consisted of four officials, who were the forerunners of a slowly growing national inspectorate. The factory acts were gradually extended to regulate the ages of working children, the hours of work and the occupations of children and women, the education of working children, and the sanitation and safety of factories and work places. Special legislation was applied to the mines and to the merchant marine, and the application of the factory acts was gradually extended from the textile factories to cover nearly all the larger establishments and many of the smaller, the so-called workshops.[10]

[6] Redlich and Hirst, *op. cit.*, p. 171.

[7] C. R. Fay, *Great Britain from Adam Smith to the Present Day*, Longmans, 1932, p. 211.

[8] *Ibid.*, p. 212.   [9] *Ibid.*, p. 213.

[10] B. L. Hutchins and A. Harrison, *A History of Factory Legislation*, London, King, 1911, Chaps. VII, VIII, and XI.

Factory legislation included a great variety of provisions aimed at sanitation and the safeguarding of health in work places. But the dangerously dirty, squalid, and disease-breeding conditions associated with the overcrowding of new urban slums required a more general control of the environment. The regulation of public health started with private bill legislation and the creation of *ad hoc* Improvement Commissioners. But a series of reports by the Poor Law Commission and by the Royal Commission of 1842-1845, and, it should be added, recurrent cholera, paved the way for several tentative general acts and finally for the Public Health Act of 1848. The Act set up a General Board of Health, which, with its inspectorate, was the forerunner of the Local Government Board established in 1871 as well as of the more recently created Ministry of Health. The Act of 1848 centralized control of water supply, sewage, drainage, and cleaning and paving of streets under any Town Councils which chose to come under its provisions and assume the powers of local sanitary authorities. It empowered the General Board of Health to create local health districts and Local Boards of Health, either on the petition of rate payers or where the annual mortality exceeded a specified rate.[11] The local authority was empowered to carry out certain duties, compelled to assume others, and clothed with the requisite financial powers. The strength of the Act was in its provision of a general health code, the partial establishment of local health authorities, and the central regulation of these authorities. Its weaknesses lay in its permissive features. Since neither the adoption of the Act by local governments nor the execution of all its provisions was wholly mandatory, its application was uneven. A generation later these weaknesses were largely overcome in the Public Health Act of 1875. Town Councils and Boards of Guardians everywhere became urban or rural sanitary authorities, their duties were extended, and central supervision with enlarged powers was fixed in the Local Government Board, created in 1871.

The modernization of the police and of poor relief, the regulalation of factories and public health, and the extension of the postal service were the most significant developments of government activity in the nineteenth century. There were other areas of lesser importance for the size of government or in which only small beginnings were made. The statistical activities of the

[11] Redlich and Hirst, *op. cit.*, p. 141.

central government were considerably enlarged, and registrars of vital statistics, of friendly societies, and of joint stock companies appeared. A start was made on railway safety and rate regulation. On the other hand, the highways—little used except for local traffic in the railway age—were left to the neglect of the local authorities through whose districts they passed. New municipal building codes, although imperfectly administered, somewhat improved the character of new housing, but left the older slums uncleared for the attention of later decades. Many municipalities organized public operation of utilities. Apart from water supply, whose significance for health made it a common city undertaking, there were numerous municipal gas works, markets, baths, harbors, docks, ferries, and cemeteries. These experiments in "municipal Socialism" were, however, limited. No electric power, electric tramways, or motorbuses yet provided outlets for municipal enterprise. Moreover, municipal trading activities required Parliamentary sanction, and municipalities without the money or the energy to obtain the necessary powers by private bills were still restrained by their limited authority from establishing municipal utility concerns.

One great area of state action still little developed by 1890 was public education. Since 1833 the central government had made grants of increasing size to help support and encourage the voluntary church schools.[12] These were maintained by associations sponsored, on the one side, by partisans of the Established Church, and, on the other, by members of the various dissenting groups. The subsidies were the lever by which central government inspection and an educational code were imposed on the private schools, a development which did much to raise the standards of primary education. By 1858, when the Newcastle Commission began its work, nearly three times as many pupils, in proportion to the population, were attending school as in 1833.[13] Still, only 19 per cent of the school children were over

[12] The early grants were miserly. "Not long after Queen Victoria came to the throne Prussia was spending £600,000 annually on public education. England in the same year, as Brougham bitterly said, voted £30,000 for education—and £70,000 for building royal stables. That spirit still lingered up to the late 'sixties . . ." (J. L. Garvin, *The Life of Joseph Chamberlain*, London, Macmillan, 1932, Vol. I, p. 89).

[13] H. C. Barnard, *Short History of English Education from 1760 to 1944*, London, University of London Press, 1947, pp. 126-127.

eleven, attendance was voluntary, brief,[14] and subject to fee, and the education given was judged inadequate even by the standards of that day. The nearly universal antipathy to a purely secular education combined with the rivalry of the various religious groups to delay a comprehensive state scheme.

The matter was brought to a head by the reform bill of 1867, which gave the urban householder a vote and marked the beginnings of a democratic franchise. "We must at least persuade our future masters to learn their letters" was an influential Parliamentary reaction.[15] The National Education League, started and led by Joseph Chamberlain, mobilized the Non-conformist sentiment of the country.[16] The fundamental step was finally taken in the Education Act of 1870. Boroughs and parishes became school districts. The Education Department, created by the government in 1856, was enjoined to set up elected school boards as *ad hoc* local education authorities in all districts where existing accommodations were deficient. The boards were empowered to establish and maintain public elementary schools as charges on the local rates, aided by government grants and school fees.[17] School attendance was still not made compulsory—that step, for children between five and ten, was taken nationally only in 1880, but many localities had already gone further. Nor were fees discarded till 1891, although school boards were empowered to remit the fees "in the case of any child when they are of the opinion that the parent of such child is unable from poverty to pay the same." Both church and board (that is, local authority) schools grew rapidly under the provisions of the Act of 1870, and the board schools established a rising standard in equipment and efficiency. So far as it depended on government, however, virtually all the advance was at an elementary level. Secondary education and technical education were largely neglected by the state before 1890.

Changes in the Size and Composition of Government Employment

The net impact of all these developments on the size of gov-

[14] *Ibid.*, pp. 127-128. Over 38 per cent of the pupils of 1858 attended for less than one year.

[15] This was Robert Lowe's well-known statement. He had opposed the reform bill but saw the need for educating the newly enfranchised workers.

[16] Garvin, *op. cit.*, Chaps. VI and VII.

[17] Barnard, *op. cit.*, pp. 135-136.

ernment in Great Britain is not easily measured. The general drift of the data, however, strongly suggests that governments in Britain not only grew over the course of the century, but increased somewhat in proportion to the growing labor force or the rising national income. In consequence, by 1890, when our tables begin, government had already attained a considerable stature.

Somewhat incomplete Census data enable us to follow the development of government employment from 1851. At that time the number of persons classified by the Census as attached to government was 254,000. Over 70 per cent of the total were in the armed forces, 17 per cent were civilian employees of the central government, and only 12 per cent were local government workers. By 1891, this incomplete total had grown to 412,000. The defense forces grew more slowly than the total and were now only 61 per cent of the whole. Civilians in the national government were 22 per cent and local government employees 17 per cent of the total. According to these figures, governments used 2.4 per cent of the labor force in 1851 and 2.8 per cent in 1891. But the categories of government workers which are missed by the Censuses of that era (for example, teachers and public utility employees) increased very swiftly in these decades, so that the relative growth of government, particularly of local government, was probably more rapid than these figures indicate. Our revision of the Census figures for 1891 suggests that government's share in the labor force was about 3.6 per cent in that year,[18] compared with the 2.8 per cent derived from the unrevised data. We doubt that a similar revision for 1851 would require so large an increase in government's share.[19]

[18] See below, note 21.

[19] Expenditure data confirm the substantial growth of government in the nineteenth century. Sidney Buxton's compilations of central government spending start in 1791, when total gross expenditures were about £ 18 million. By 1886, when his figures end, they were £ 94 million, a fivefold increase. They were almost the same in 1890, according to Bernard Mallet. Compilations of aggregate local expenditures are available only since 1867, when some £ 32 million was spent, net of the contributions of the central government. By 1891 this sum had nearly doubled; it stood at over £ 63 million.

By 1890 the three great categories of central government expenditure—the debt service, military expenses, and all other expenditure—were of roughly the same order of magnitude. But in reaching this rough equality, the debt service had grown only some two and one-half times during the preceding century, military expenses had increased about five times, and

Apart from the armed forces and the East Indian Civil Service, the chief employers of labor in the nineteenth century governmental service are easily identified. Of the 40,000-odd civilian employees of the central government as reported by the Census in 1851, over 25 per cent were in the Post Office, nearly 40 per cent were engaged in inland revenue and customs collection, and another 20 per cent were messengers and workers in the dockyards and ordnance factories. Of the remaining 5,600 persons, nearly 1,000 were peers, MP's, and attachés of the Royal Court and some 2,000 were civilians in the military and naval departments. Indeed the special Census return of 1851 shows only 1,628 persons engaged in the civil departments of the government for general administrative purposes. Some of the departments administering important new departures in government were ludicrously small. The Board of Trade had 103 employees, including

---

other expenses, which reflect the new functions of government in an industrial community, had increased over ten times. (A different classification of expenditures has been adopted by Alan Peacock in his forthcoming study. His figures, therefore, will not agree exactly with these. See Chapter 1, note 1, above.) In the local sphere the big increases during the quarter century covered by our figures were in municipal sanitation and public works and in education. By 1891 the first category had grown to nearly three times its size in 1867. The second had increased from zero to £ 8,227,000 and amounted to 11.5 per cent of local expenditures.

If we compare these figures with the crude estimates for national income assembled by Lord Stamp from various sources, we find that central government expenditures were some 8 per cent of the national income in 1791. Excluding the debt service, the percentage is only 4 per cent. In 1890 the percentage is 7.3 per cent including debt service, 5.3 per cent excluding it. Central and local expenditures together were 10.7 per cent of national income in 1867 (7.4 per cent excluding national debt service); in 1890 they were about 12 per cent of the national income (about 10 per cent after excluding national debt service charges). The national income figures cited in Lord Stamp's book are not well defined and the significance of our percentages is correspondingly ambiguous. Based on the more precisely defined Jefferys-Walters estimates of national income at factor cost, the 1890 total expenditures, including debt service, were 11 per cent of national income. These are tentative estimates of national income and may be revised by their authors before publication.

See Sidney Buxton, *Finance and Politics*, London, Murray, 1888, Vol. II, Appendix G; Bernard Mallet, *British Budgets, 1887-88 to 1912-13*, London, Macmillan, 1913, Table II, pp. 476-477; *Statistical Abstract for the United Kingdom*, 1898, Tables 19 and 20, pp. 40-43; J. C. Stamp, *British Incomes and Property*, London, King, 1916, p. 427; James B. Jefferys and Dorothy Walters, "National Income and Expenditure of the United Kingdom, 1870-1952," mimeographed, a paper submitted to the International Association for Research in Income and Wealth, Third Conference, Castel Gandolfo, September 1953.

24 office-keepers, messengers, and porters. There were 23 inspectors of factories and mines. The Poor Law Board employed 84 and the newly established General Board of Health only 30 persons.[20]

The distribution of local government workers in 1851 was also heavily concentrated in certain departments. Some 59 per cent of the local civil service consisted of policemen. Some 17 per cent more were magistrates, sheriff's officers, and prison officials, leaving only 24 per cent for the other functions of local government. It should be remembered, however, that the 1851 Census excludes certain categories of employees—particularly workers directly employed on local construction projects.

The departmental distribution of central government employment did not alter much in the second half of the Victorian era. Post Office, inland revenue, and customs collection continued to dominate civilian government employment. On the surface the Census figures suggest that the situation in local governments was also basically unchanged. The police rose slightly, from 59 to 62 per cent of total local employment. The remainder of the local government servants dropped from 41 to 38 per cent. However, the workers employed in those government services missed by the Census were increasing, so that the Census figures alone tell a misleading story. Teachers and others in the new public school system and the burgeoning numbers of municipal utilities workers were swelling the public payrolls. The police forces, in all probability, no longer included more than 30 per cent of the people on local government payrolls. Functions other than mere security were now accounting for increased employment.[21]

Political and Ideological Brakes on the Expansion of Government

In the nineteenth century the British people began to adapt their government to the social problems raised by the progress of industrialization and urban concentration and by the capitalistic economic organization within which these processes occurred. But compared with the rapid sweep of industrialization in the nineteenth century or with the rapidity of government

[20] The older agencies were also thinly manned. The Foreign Office had 85, the Colonial Office 49, and the Treasury 96 employees and officials. *Census of Population, 1851*, House of Commons, Accounts and Papers, 1852-1853, Vol. LXXVIII, pp. CCCXLIX-CCCL.

expansion in the twentieth, the growth of government in the 1800's was slow. It is not to be understood, therefore, in terms of the impact of the new economic forces alone. The political

21 The discussion in the text is based on the following table of employment (in thousands of persons):

	1851, Census	1891, Census	1891, Adjusted
Armed forces at home and abroad	178.8	249.0	249.0
National civil government	40.3	90.6	105.0-115.0
Peers, MP's, members of the Royal Court, etc.	0.9		
Post Office	10.4		
Inland revenue and customs	15.9		
Other civil servants in administrative and military departments	4.6		
Messengers and workmen	3.4		
Dockyard artificers and laborers	5.0		
East India Service	3.8	0.2	
Local government	31.0	72.0	150.0-200.0
Police	18.3	44.7	44.7
Others	12.6	27.3	105.0-155.0
Total government	253.9	411.8	504.0-564.0
Labor force	10,447.0	14,682.0	14,682.0
Government workers as per cent of labor force	2.4	2.8	3.4-3.8

Sources

1851: *Census of Population, 1851,* House of Commons, Accounts and Papers, 1852-1853, Vol. LXXXVIII, Table 54. Labor force includes persons of specified occupations or status less housewives, children not seeking work, persons of rank, inmates of asylums, etc., plus armed forces abroad.

This table includes only those employees whose principal occupation was in government work. A special canvass of central government departments, which covered all those wholly or partly employed, gave a total of male workers in Great Britain some 10,400 larger than did the Census tables proper (*ibid.,* pp. CCCXLIX-CCCL). The difference lay almost entirely in the Post Office and among the "artificers and laborers" of the Admiralty. The discrepancy in the Post Office was due to the large number of sub-postmasters and sub-postmistresses whose chief occupation was not in the postal service. The discrepancy in the Admiralty may have occurred partly because workers whose major occupation was outside government were included, but presumably also because in an occupational census many manual workers are classified only by their occupation but not grouped under the industry of their employer. They were, therefore, not included under government in the regular Census tables.

1891: See Tables 1, 2, and 8 and "Sources and Notes to Tables and Charts." Census figures omit industrial workers, teachers, etc. Adjusted figures include them.

19

and ideological environment of the time was an important conditioning factor which tended to check the expansion of governmental activity, so that the full impact of many problems which appeared before 1900 was not felt until the present century.

One retarding factor was the distribution of political power. Not till 1884 was universal householder suffrage achieved, and even that was not universal male suffrage. And since the English were, as Walter Bagehot said, a "deferential nation," and since labor political organization did not achieve any real power until decades after the vote was secured, effective control remained firmly in the grip of the gentry and the business classes.[22]

The views of these classes were, therefore, embodied in governmental policy with but little dilution or concession. During most of the century the political policies of these groups were heavily influenced by a popularized and somewhat corrupt version of the doctrines of individualism and of governmental non-interference, of which the writings of Bentham and the classical economists were the purer intellectual foundation.[23] These doctrines, besides helping to remove the older mercantilist controls, did indeed support the various Reform Acts of the 1830's, the further extension of the franchise, and the establishment of a modern civil service. They thus helped lay the political and administrative bases for an extension of governmental activity at a later stage. It is also important to remember that Bentham and his economist allies were not unqualifiedly and universally averse to state action. They saw at least two great positive duties for government in economic life: the first, to protect those classes of individuals who were not sufficiently enlightened or responsible to act for themselves; the second, to erect and maintain ". . . certain public works and certain public institutions, which

[22] See D. C. Somervell, *British Politics since 1900*, London, Dakers, 1950, p. 21.

[23] The general acceptance of individualism by the leading elements of all political parties in the era between the Reform Bills of 1832 and 1867 is described by A. V. Dicey, *Lectures on the Relation between Law and Public Opinion in England during the Nineteenth Century*, London, Macmillan, 1905, pp. 176-183.

"What then was the extent to which the Benthamism of common sense or individualism, obtained acceptance?

"The answer may be given with certainty and decision. From 1832 onwards the supremacy of individualism among the classes then capable of influencing legislation was for many years incontestable and patent" (*ibid.*, p. 176).

it can never be for the interest of any individual, or small number of individuals, to erect and maintain; because the profit could never repay the expense to any individual or small number of individuals, though it may frequently do much more than repay it to a great society."[24] Their conception of the first duty, for example, caused many, though not all, classical economists to favor the regulation of children's work in factories; but fewer of them favored the extension of factory regulation to women and none to men.[25] Their conception of the scope of the second duty led Bentham and the economists to favor public provision of sanitation and hospital services and of elementary education.[26]

In spite of these qualifications of principle, it seems fair to say that, during the heyday of its influence, the markedly individualistic tenor of utilitarian and economic theory, when translated into the sphere of practical politics, interposed a steady check upon governmental action. For this at least three reasons may plausibly be advanced. One is that the popularized versions of political economy confined the role of the state within far narrower limits than did the original. Another is that even where a modern individualist might see an occasion for state action under one or the other of the principles just stated, a nineteenth century individualist saw none, either because his conception of the capabilities of the state was more limited or because he was so intent to encourage the spirit of self-help and independence. And still a third reason is that the predominant influence of the business class, as contrasted with that of the working class, in the government made for a strict application of individualistic doctrine. They conceived their country's interests as well as their own to lie in freedom from governmental restraint and in strict governmental economy.

The more far-reaching practical significance of the role which Bentham and the classical economists assigned the state may,

[24] The significant areas within which the classical political economists and Bentham approved state action in spite of their general disposition to rely on individual action are well set out by Lionel Robbins in *The Theory of Economic Policy*, London, Macmillan, 1952. The quotation in the text is from Adam Smith's *Wealth of Nations* and is cited by Robbins (*op. cit.*, p. 37).

[25] Robbins, *op. cit.*, p. 102.

[26] It is significant, however, that as late as 1859, John Stuart Mill "deprecated the direct assumption by the State of educational functions, and contended that it ought to do no more than compel parents to provide for the elementary education of their children" (Dicey, *op. cit.*, p. 276).

therefore, be chiefly that it provided a reasoned basis for state action, within the dominant ideological tradition, for use in later decades.[27] At the time, however, such prominent cases of governmental intervention as the Factories Acts gained support in part because they appealed to the humanitarian spirit prominent in English religious feeling, just as the movement for sanitation and municipal facilities appealed to both the humanitarian and business instincts, not to say the sense of sheer expediency, of the ruling groups in Parliament and in the city governments. But all these influences gained such ground as they did against the steady opposition of a strong anti-interventionist current.[28]

These political and philosophic influences were bolstered by outward circumstances. The nineteenth century was a century which, for many purposes of historical analysis, began with the Congress of Vienna and ran until the assassination at Sarajevo. It was a period in which the relative absence of large-scale war left trade channels undisturbed and foreign investments secure. Since the economic adjustments to be made at any one time were usually minor, the forces of the market had an unparalleled chance to perform to the general satisfaction the functions of economic organization and control. When the aged Sir William Harcourt could say to the youthful Churchill, "My dear Winston . . . , the experiences of a long life have convinced me that nothing ever happens,"[29] governments, and particularly the British government, might well feel absolved from the need to do much to encourage or restrain the enterprise of individuals or to offset the results of their bargains.

But the minor role of government during the nineteenth cen-

[27] Robbins, *op. cit.*, p. 37.

[28] As to the opposition of Benthamite liberalism to, and the support of humanitarianism for, the Factories Acts, see Dicey (*op. cit.*, pp. 108 and 219-239). As already noted, there were many classical economists who supported factory regulation, at least for children. Dicey also considered that the assumption of state responsibility for public education was delayed by the "distrust of State intervention which characterized the Benthamite era" (*ibid.*, p. 276). The inter-city competition which supported the improvement of municipal facilities is described by Fay (*op. cit.*, pp. 156-158). The convenience and expediency of using local government to do jobs which, in one way or another, demanded doing, are suggested by R. C. K. Ensor (*England, 1870-1914*, Oxford, 1936, p. 128).

[29] Winston Churchill, *The World Crisis*, Scribner's, 1931, p. 15. The year was 1895, the year of the Jameson raid. German naval ambitions were soon to be made manifest, and, as Churchill says, "Since that moment, as it seems to me, nothing has ever ceased happening."

tury reflects more than the absence of violent economic disruption; it also reflects the infancy of the economic and social sciences. Compared with recent decades, the volume of systematic information about social conditions was very small, which meant that the existence of problems was hard to establish persuasively. Moreover, even when a problem was sufficiently obtrusive, often no plausible means of solving it could be seen. The responsibility of governments for corrective action, therefore, was not recognized. If the volume of unemployment is unknown, the gravity of the problem is in doubt. If its connection with the state of business at large is not understood, it can be attributed to the personal failings of individual workers. If there is no plausible method of counteracting or avoiding economic fluctuations by social action, no responsibility falls upon the government. Unemployment due to business cycles has been characteristic of industrial capitalism since at least 1750, but not until the early 1900's was the connection clearly established, and even then the volume of unemployment was not yet accurately measured. It was not until the 1930's that social remedies for depression were offered which gained widespread support. The assumption of broad government responsibility for economic stabilization was therefore delayed almost to the present time. What was true of business cycles was true of many problems thrown up by industrialism and capitalism in the last century. With few exceptions, the social studies which were the necessary prelude to state action were not completed, in some cases not even begun, before 1900. For all these reasons the last century was a time only of great beginnings in the growth of government. More recent decades have witnessed the rapid acceleration of that growth.

CHAPTER 3

THE BRITISH GOVERNMENT SINCE 1890:
A GENERAL VIEW

IN THE nineteenth century the British government's absorption of labor increased markedly, but there is little to indicate that labor employed by government grew much more rapidly than did the country's population. As the century drew to a close, however, the pace of governmental growth spurted, and, apart from fluctuations connected with war, the fraction of the labor force employed by the state increased rapidly—an increase unbroken to the present time.

From 1891 to 1950, government employment increased from less than 4 to nearly 14 per cent of the labor force (see Table 1). These figures exclude all nationalized industries and public services other than the Post Office. If nationalized industries and services are included, the 1950 percentage rises to 24. Thus toward the end of the nineteenth century, one worker in twenty-five was on a government payroll. In the middle of the twentieth century, one in seven was working in a regular government agency and nearly one in four either in such an agency or in a nationalized industry or service.

To obtain these figures and those for intervening decades, we were able to use the excellent Census data for 1911, 1921, and 1931. Before 1911 the Census data are incomplete. Small revisions, which we describe in subsequent chapters, were required to make good the deficiencies in the Census figures for the central government in these early years. Very large revisions had to be made in the local government figures. Since 1931 there has been no complete Census of government workers,[1] but the Ministry of Labour manpower series, taken together with the Treasury returns for the civil service, make fair estimates possible for 1938 and later years. For 1950 we have made use of an estimate by T. M. Ridley of the British Central Statistical Office, who based

---

[1] The 1941 Census was omitted because of the war. The final results of the 1951 Census were not yet available at time of writing. It was known, however, that this latest Census did not distinguish between private and public employment, but allocated government workers, as far as possible, to their proper industrial groups. An estimate of central government employment based upon preliminary figures from the 1951 Census is included in Table 2. See Chapter 4.

TABLE 1

Total Government Employment and Working Population, Selected Years, 1891-1950

	THOUSANDS OF EMPLOYED AND UNEMPLOYED PERSONS (FULL-TIME AND PART-TIME)					PER CENT OF ALL GOVT. WORKERS[a]			PER CENT OF TOTAL WORKING POPULATION[a]			
	Armed Forces[b]	Civil Central Govt.	Local Govt.	Total Govt.	Total Working Population	Armed Forces[b]	Civil Central Govt.	Local Govt.	Armed Forces[b]	Civil Central Govt.	Local Govt.	Total Govt.
1891	249	105-115	150-200	504-564	14,682	46.6	20.6	32.8	1.7	0.7	1.2	3.6
1901	423	155-165	350-400	928-988	16,605	44.2	16.7	39.1	2.5	1.0	2.3	5.8
1911	343	271	660	1,274	18,509	26.9	21.3	51.8	1.8	1.5	3.6	6.9
1921	475	508	976	1,959	19,604	24.3	25.9	49.8	2.4	2.6	5.0	10.0
1931	360	441	1,263	2,064	21,256	17.4	21.4	61.2	1.7	2.1	5.9	9.7
1938	385	581	1,273	2,239	22,604	17.2	25.9	56.9	1.7	2.6	5.6	9.9
1950	690	1,102	1,422	3,214	23,068	21.5	34.3	44.2	3.0	4.8	6.2	13.9
1950c	690	3,485	1,422	5,597	23,068	12.3	62.3	25.4	3.0	15.1	6.2	24.3

	THOUSANDS OF EMPLOYED PERSONS (FULL-TIME AND PART-TIME)					PER CENT OF ALL EMPLOYED GOVT. WORKERS			PER CENT OF ALL EMPLOYED WORKERS			
	Armed Forces[b]	Civil Central Govt.	Local Govt.	All Employed Govt.	All Employed	Armed Forces[b]	Civil Central Govt.	Local Govt.	Armed Forces[b]	Civil Central Govt.	Local Govt.	All Employed Govt.
1931	354	423	1,153	1,930	18,731	18.3	21.9	59.8	1.9	2.3	6.2	10.3
1938	385	581	1,273	2,239	20,619	17.2	25.9	56.9	1.9	2.8	6.2	10.9
1950	690	1,102	1,422	3,214	22,787	21.5	34.3	44.2	3.0	4.9	6.2	14.1
1950c	690	3,485	1,422	5,597	22,787	12.3	62.3	25.4	3.0	15.3	6.2	24.6

a Percentages based upon the mid-points of the ranges in 1891 and 1901.

b Includes armed forces abroad.

c Including nationalized industries and services employing 2,383,000 persons.

See "Sources and Notes to Tables and Charts" for sources of this and other tables and charts.

his figures on Ministry of Labour information, both published and unpublished. The figures for the armed forces are sufficiently accurate for our purposes throughout the sixty-year period. Our methods of estimate are set out in some detail in the appendix notes to Table 1 and subsequent tables.

In 1891 the chief function of British government, as measured by its use of manpower, was national defense: nearly 50 per cent of the men hired by government were in the armed forces. About 20 per cent were in the civilian branches of the central government. Somewhat over 30 per cent were local government employees. In the next sixty years, however, while the armed forces nearly tripled, the central civilian departments, including those supporting the armed forces, grew to about ten times, and the local governments to over eight times, their former size. In 1950 the armed forces accounted for only 22 per cent of government employment; civilian employees of the central government amounted to 34 per cent; and local government workers to 44 per cent. In addition, the workers in the nationalized industries were about as numerous as were the civilians in the central and local governments combined. Of the 2.7 million persons, more or less, who were added to the government's rolls (apart from the nationalized industries) between 1890 and 1950, about 440,000 went into the armed forces, about 1 million were civilians in the central government, and some 1,250,000 were added to local government staffs.

During this period in which the total working population of Great Britain grew from 14.7 to 23.1 million persons—an increase of 57 per cent—government employment, nationalized industries apart, increased 450 to 500 per cent. No other single major industry which can be followed over the entire period grew so fast. Over 30 per cent of the net addition to the working population during the sixty-year period was required by a governmental agency for work in some capacity. Between 1931 and 1950, over 60 per cent of the additional workers were so absorbed. (See Charts 1 and 2 for a summary of this growth.)

There is a variety of causes for the phenomenal growth which these figures reveal. During most of the nineteenth century, the expansion of government in response to the many problems created by the industrialization of production, by the concomitant rise of city life, and by the dependence of economic activity

CHART 1

Number of Government and Other Public Workers (including Military Personnel) by Main Types of Governmental Unit, Selected Years, 1891-1950

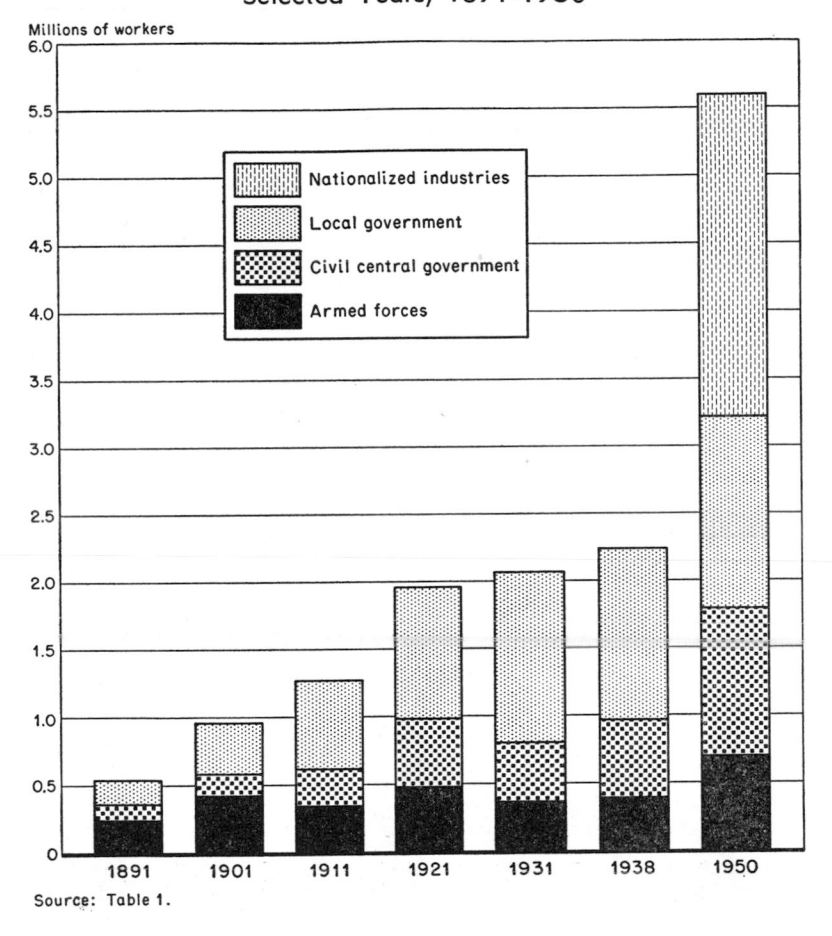

Source: Table 1.

on the operation of distant and unstable markets, was checked, though far from wholly prevented, by a set of forces described in Chapter 2. But in the last decades of the century these checks began to weaken, and in the course of time they were largely reversed and replaced by powerful influences favoring the growth of government.

One of these checks, limited suffrage, was partly eliminated by the extension of voting power to the working classes by the

27

CHART 2

Government and Other Public Workers as a Percentage of the Labor Force, Selected Years, 1891-1950

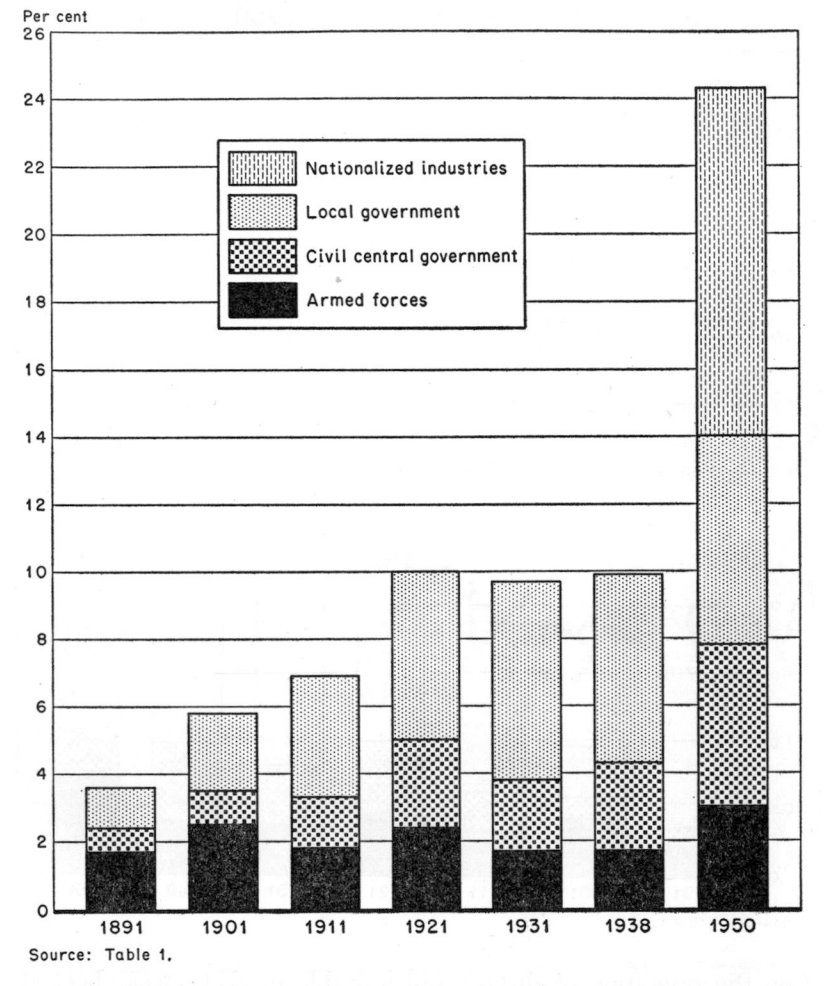

Source: Table 1.

Acts of 1867 and 1884.[2] Years were required, however, for the power latent in these Acts to be harnessed for practical political action. Although working class members—"Lib-Labs"—began to appear in the House of Commons as early as 1874, not till 1900

[2] These Acts enfranchised householders in town and country. Universal male suffrage was not achieved until 1918, when women over 30 also were given the vote subject to certain property qualifications. Finally, in 1928 the franchise was extended to all women 21 years of age and over.

was there a concerted effort to elect Labour members under the aegis of the newly founded Labour Representation Committee. Within the older parties, in the 1870's and 1880's, Randolph Churchill, with his vision of a Tory Democracy, and Joseph Chamberlain and his Radical allies began the process of adapting political programs to the demands of a mass electorate. Patriotic sentiment aroused by the issues of Irish home rule, colonial expansion, and the Boer War, however, kept social reform in the shade for a long stretch, and not till late 1905 did the Liberals return to office newly equipped with an active program and a vigorous leadership pledged to further intervention by government in economic life. In the election of January 1906, moreover, 29 Labour members and 14 members of the Miners' Federation were elected, and from that time the influence of workers' demands on government became continuous and strong.

Coincident with this beginning of the shift of voting power, the prevailing view of the proper functions of the state widened. Benthamite individualism began to suffer the penalties of its own triumph. During most of the nineteenth century, the problem of social progress had presented itself to enlightened men as one of freeing the individual drive for self-advancement from the trammels of state control. This liberation had been largely achieved, with extraordinary results in Great Britain. But not all the results had been satisfactory, and people with humanitarian impulses began to ask whether the state might not be used to mitigate some of the evils with which the success of liberated trade was mixed. In this the humanitarians were aided by the Benthamite doctrine itself. This taught that individual liberty was, in general, the proper means for ensuring the objectives of society. More fundamentally, however, it taught that the object of social arrangements is the greatest happiness of the greatest number. And in those sectors where it now appeared that the object might be better achieved by collective action, it was clear that individualism would give way.[3] By 1891 the Birmingham Radical businessman Joseph Chamberlain could argue in the House of Commons that "the State is justified in passing any law,

[3] A. V. Dicey, *Lectures on the Relation between Law and Public Opinion in England during the Nineteenth Century*, London, Macmillan, 1905, pp. 302-309; Lionel Robbins, *The Theory of Economic Policy*, London, Macmillan, 1952, pp. 36-46; and pp. 20-22, above.

or even in doing any single act, which in its ulterior consequences added to the sum of human happiness."[4]

Side by side with this transition in orthodox opinion, a more comprehensive Socialist view had been gaining ground. This view was little accepted in 1890, but it was already being actively propagated. Its adherents became the intellectual leaders of the British Labour Party, and it has come to be a strong force in British political life.

The accumulation of factual information about social conditions and the development of economics and the social sciences increased the pressure for government intervention. In the first place, while great progress had been made through industrialization in a regime of individualism, a very large portion of the British population continued to live in conditions which, by slowly rising standards, were considered impoverished. Surveys like Charles Booth's *Life and Labour of the People in London* revealed conditions which shocked public opinion in the late eighties and nineties.[5] As statistics improved and students of social conditions multiplied, the continued existence of such conditions was kept before the public. Increasing knowledge of them aroused influential circles and furnished working class movements with factual weapons. Second, from the last part of the nineteenth century, the rising social sciences tended to stress the social or systemic, rather than the personal, origins of misfortune. When Beatrice Webb, as one of Booth's investigators, found that disorganized hiring methods maintained in partial employment on the London docks several times as many men as could be kept in steady work, she was pointing to a social cause of unemployment and poverty. When Sir William Beveridge was led to attach to his early book on *Unemployment* (1909)

[4] J. L. Garvin, *Life of Joseph Chamberlain*, London, Macmillan, 1932, Vol. II, p. 534. Cited in J. H. Clapham, *An Economic History of Modern Britain*, Vol. III, p. 397. Clapham comments: "This was a view which Chamberlain, the Radical Unionist, shared with Randolph Churchill, the Tory Democrat; with Robert Blatchford the Socialist, and with a great number of plain men labelled or unlabelled."

[5] The results of Booth's first studies were published in a series of papers in the *Journal of the Royal Statistical Society* beginning in 1886. The report of his pioneer survey of London appeared in preliminary form as *Labour and Life of the People* in 1889 and 1891. His elaborate final report in 18 volumes, *Life and Labour of the People in London*, was published in 1902. B. S. Rowntree's similar survey of York, *Poverty; A Study of Town Life*, was published in 1901.

the subtitle *A Problem of Industry*, he was shifting the burden of responsibility from the shoulders of the individual to those of society. Third, the development of economic science increasingly undercut the Victorian conviction that such maladjustments as unemployment are evanescent or isolated phenomena and that the free market has a persistent tendency to eliminate unemployment and to allocate work and workers with satisfactory efficiency. When Keynes wrote of *The End of Laissez-Faire* in 1927, he was saying more than that governments in their folly had abandoned the policy of non-intervention, and more than that the development of monopoly and the destruction of war had made the policy less workable. He was also, and more fundamentally, arguing that the theoretical bases of laissez-faire were less solid than economists had supposed and that, in the absence of governmental management in at least some spheres, the automatic workings of the market could not be trusted to produce satisfactory results. In this conviction he was already representative of a wide section of opinion within professional economics, and his *General Theory of Employment, Interest and Money*, when it appeared a decade later, merely consolidated the triumph of this view. Since that time the weight of expert opinion has sanctioned some form or degree of systematic governmental planning in economic life.

These gradual shifts in political power, in the dominant political theory, and in social and economic science would, in themselves, no doubt have been enough to account for a far more active governmental response to the problems of industrialism and of capitalistic economic organization. In fact, however, those problems, especially in Great Britain, were enormously aggravated by other developments.

During most of the nineteenth century, Great Britain had enjoyed the advantages of her headstart in industrialization. But beginning in the last decades of that century and even more after 1900, Britain felt the impact of foreign competition in all fields in which she had previously been most secure—in engineering, and, somewhat later, in textiles and in coal. This raised a series of questions for industrial policy which, in palmier days, had been more easily avoided: protection, subsidy, rationalization, and nationalization. The pinch of foreign competition also called in question the organization of the capital markets, which seemed

31

to facilitate foreign rather than home issues. It aggravated the perennial problem of unemployment by permitting the emergence of persistent areas of depressed industry. And it complicated the maintenance of Britain's balance of international payments. For after World War I it proved impossible to expand exports of commodities and services sufficiently to cover new foreign investment. And after World War II, in the face of great losses of investment income and of an inflationary policy at home, exports were insufficient even to cover Britain's purchases abroad.

Of even greater importance, however, were the problems raised by war and defense. In contrast to the Victorian Age and its freedom from general war, the twentieth century has already witnessed two great conflicts. More than that, the progress of industry and the accumulation of capital have revolutionized the scope and character of wars and their influence on economic life. Because the capital equipment of the soldier has become many times more expensive and his consumption of munitions has multiplied, it has become necessary to mobilize vastly greater fractions of wealth and income than were formerly needed. The administrative organization controlling and supporting the fighting formations has grown apace. Modern weapons are more destructive and modern armies are capable of operating on a far larger scale at far larger distances from their homes than was true a century ago. And as economic activity, and particularly Britain's economy, has become dependent on the steady operation of distant markets, the impact of war on production and trade has been extremely severe.

As a consequence of these various changes, the size of the total defense establishment has grown faster than that of the armed forces. The actual prosecution of war has required extensive intervention by the state, and the economic problems of recovery from war have involved continued governmental activity during the interludes of peace. The elaborate regulatory agencies thus called into being constitute bureaucratic instruments which have made it easier for the state to undertake functions unconnected with war.

These many-sided developments form the general background against which the expansion of the British state in the last sixty or seventy years must be placed. In subsequent chapters we look more closely at the ways in which these various influences made themselves felt in the chief branches of government.

CHAPTER 4

THE BRITISH CENTRAL GOVERNMENT,
1890-1950

DURING the sixty years from 1890 to 1950, the number of persons in the employ of the British central government multiplied about fivefold. Some 1.4 million people were added to the armed forces and civilian staffs. The portion of the country's total labor force absorbed by the central government rose from 2.4 per cent to 7.7 per cent (Table 1 and Table 4, Part C).[1] These figures reflect only the operations of the ordinary departments of government. The impact of the newly nationalized industries is described in Chapter 6.

This great rise did not occur in an uninterrupted way. Instead, the changing pressures of international and domestic problems and politics accelerated or retarded the pace of development for many years at a time. Three quite different periods are roughly definable. In the first, from 1890 to 1914, there was fairly steady response to forces already well established in the nineteenth century. Total central government employment doubled; that of civilians roughly tripled. During the second period, from 1914 to about 1933, an explosive expansion of the structure of the state occurred during World War I and was followed by contraction. Total employment at the end of the twenty-year period was no higher than at the beginning, but the number of civilian workers was somewhat greater and the size of the armed forces somewhat smaller. The third period, roughly from 1933 to the present, included the recovery from depression, the preparation for World War II, the great efflorescence of state power in the course of the war, and its redirection—with only some reduction—in the period since the war.

FROM 1890 TO 1914

Compared with the storms of later decades, the years from 1890 to World War I were quiet. The British economy, though not booming, was prosperous. Average real wage rates rose

[1] The absolute increase from 1891 to 1951, as shown by the adjusted Census data in Table 2, was 1,578,000 persons; the share of the labor force in 1951 was 8.5 per cent.

TABLE 2

Central Government Full-Time and Part-Time Employment as Shown by Census Data, 1891-1951

	1891	1901	1911	1921	1931	1951c
			Thousands of Persons			
Armed forces[a]	249.0	422.7	342.8	475.2	359.7	826.7
Non-industrial civilian employees	90.8	130.0	229.9	410.7	372.1	783.0
Post Office, total	n.a.	n.a.	142.0	211.1	228.5	330.3
Other	n.a.	n.a.	87.9	199.6	143.6	452.7
Industrial workers	20.0[b]	30.0[b]	41.5	97.6	68.5	328.2
Total	359.8	582.7	614.2	983.5	800.3	1,937.9
			Per Cent of Total			
Armed forces[a]	69.2	72.5	55.8	48.3	44.9	42.7
Non-industrial civilian employees	25.2	22.3	37.4	41.8	46.5	40.4
Post Office, total	n.a.	n.a.	23.1	21.5	28.6	17.0
Other	n.a.	n.a.	14.3	20.3	17.9	23.4
Industrial workers	5.6[b]	5.1[b]	6.8	9.9	8.6	16.9
Total	100.0	100.0	100.0	100.0	100.0	100.0
Total as percentage of working population	2.4	3.5	3.3	5.0	3.8	8.5

a Includes armed forces abroad.
b Estimate; not available in Census.
c See "Sources and Notes to Tables and Charts" for sources of 1951 data.

generally during the 1890's and then, with many differences among trades, and with some fluctuations, remained about on a level from 1900 to 1913. Unemployment rates were generally low.[2] Agriculture, after ruinous years in the 1880's and early 1890's when the impact of foreign competition was severe, enjoyed a period of mild recovery.

In international affairs it was a time of colonial rivalries and of diplomatic maneuvers climaxed by the Great War, the outbreak of which we use as the terminal date of the period. For Britain it included both the minor, but serious, conflict with the Boers and the pressure of German naval rivalry. Many influences, therefore, combined to force a strengthening of the armed forces.

In domestic politics, the Irish question, which caused the Liberal split in 1886, was very much to the fore. Although, as already noted, this split helped keep the Conservatives—with dissident Liberal support—in power until 1905, there was an interlude of Liberal government from 1892 to 1895. Moreover, the dissidents who joined the Tories over Home Rule were not only conservative Whigs but also Radical Unionists, led by Joseph Chamberlain. Still more, the political constitution of the country was changing in a manner which favored economic and social reform. A mass electorate had been created, labor unions made rapid progress in the 1890's, and Labour representation and Labour political activity both increased. Socialist propaganda and organization became more widespread and Socialist theory more widely accepted.

In these conditions the numbers employed by the central government approximately doubled, rising from about 360,000, as indicated by the Census data of Table 2, to about 720,000, as shown by the not quite comparable departmental figures of Table 4, Part A. As a share of the labor force, the increase was from 2.4 per cent to 3.8 per cent.

The details of the change are, unfortunately, obscure in certain respects. The Census categories are very broad and therefore unrevealing. The government itself had not yet compiled consolidated statements of the total numbers on its payrolls arranged by function or department. However, data for established civil servants[3] in certain years, which we have arranged in Table 3,

[2] J. H. Clapham, *An Economic History of Modern Britain*, London, Cambridge University Press, 1938, Vol. III, pp. 464-471.

[3] An established civil servant is one who is admitted to the permanent

help piece out the picture. With these data and collateral information, a number of developments of wide significance may be discerned.

The outstanding fact is that the bulk of the increase in governmental employment is accounted for by defense activities and by the Post Office. The armed forces increased from about 250,000 in 1891 to 395,000 on the eve of World War I.[4] It was, moreover, an era of modernization and expansion in the equipment and organization of the Army and Navy. The Navy's main battle fleets were rebuilt three times in response to revolutionary advances in guns, armor, and means of propulsion—once in the late 1880's and early 1890's (Lord George Hamilton's program), again in the 1890's (Lord Spencer's program), and still again after 1905, when the Fisher-Cawdor program gave Britain its fleet of dreadnoughts and super-dreadnoughts. All this effort was hastened under the spur of German naval rivalry.[5]

The Army's long-standing deficiencies in organization and equipment were at last taken in hand as a result of its scandalously poor showing in the Boer War. By the Haldane reforms of 1906-1909, it was expanded, reorganized at the top and in the field, and provided with more modern arms and a more adequate outfit of transport, medical, and other auxiliary equipment.[6]

The net result was a very large expansion in the defense ministries and in the number of industrial workers employed in government dockyards and arsenals. Our estimate is that this accounted for an increase of some 50,000 or 60,000 workers (cf. Table 2, 1891, and Table 4, Part A, 1914).

Another large part of the increase occurred in the Post Office. The annual reports of the Postmaster General show an increase

---

civil service with a certificate from the Civil Service Commissioners and who otherwise holds a position entitling him eventually to a superannuation allowance. (Cf. *Introductory Memoranda Relating to the Civil Service*, submitted by the Treasury to the Royal Commission on the Civil Service, Appendix I to Part I of Minutes of Evidence, 1930, p. 1.) Unestablished personnel are of particular importance among Post Office workers and industrial staff.

[4] This compares a Census figure in 1891 with one derived from departmental reports in 1914. The strength as compiled from departmental sources was 276,000 in 1891.

[5] R. C. K. Ensor, *England, 1870-1914*, Oxford, 1936, pp. 177, 286-289, and 363-365.

[6] *Ibid.*, pp. 292-293, 395-396, and 525.

TABLE 3

Central Government Employment,
Established Civil Service Only,
1902, 1911, 1914

Departmental Groups	Mar. 31, 1902	Mar. 31, 1911	Mar. 31, 1914
Defense and supply	9,908	10,637	12,363
Admiralty	8,869	9,248	10,948
War Office	1,039	1,389	1,415
Post Office	77,035	99,355	123,668
Revenue departments	9,265	10,682	11,955
Inland Revenue	5,388	2,669	3,259
Customs and Excise	3,877	8,013	8,696
Social services	2,173	2,821	5,331
Education	1,614	2,093	2,200
Local Government Board	463	623	708
Insurance	0	0	2,249
Friendly Societies Register and others	96	105	174
Trade, industry, and transport	1,320	1,967	3,167
Board of Agriculture and Fisheries	181	349	634
Office of Woods and Forests	46	53	63
Board of Trade	1,093	1,565	2,470
Agency services	800	1,639	1,924
Ordnance survey	205	887	926
Mint	188	199	220
Stationery Office	87	134	191
Public works	320	419	587
Home and legal departments	5,147	5,907	6,271
Central Government and Finance	470	485	515
Home Office and legal departments	1,474	1,732	2,058
Prison Commission	3,203	3,690	3,698
Foreign and imperial services	240	285	303
Colonial Office	113	138	145
Foreign Office	127	147	158
Total	105,888	133,293	164,982

Note: The staffs of specifically named Irish departments have been eliminated. But certain departments, notably the Post Office and Revenue Departments, include Irish workers who could not be excluded.

in staff of 122,000—from 106,000 to 228,000 workers.[7] The expansion reflects an enormous increase in the volume of ordinary

[7] These figures include established and other employees of the Post Office, some of whom were part-time workers. They exclude employees in Ireland and overseas.

postal business and an expansion in postal savings and in telegraph activity. In this period, too, the Post Office's participation in the growing telephone business gradually increased until, in 1912, it absorbed the entire national system.

Other departments of the central government also grew rapidly —not the revenue departments, which were almost as large in 1851 as in 1914, but the departments in charge of regulating and guiding industry and trade, administering the new social services, and controlling the growing body of local officials and functions in the fields of health and education. The Board of Agriculture was strengthened as an information agency and given new administrative powers in connection with a law which radically changed the relation of landlord and tenant. The Board of Trade's powers over railroads were increased. The Home Office and the Local Government Board were enlarged to deal with the host of local officials required under the new local government acts of the late 1880's and early 1890's. Factory legislation went forward. The Board of Education was established in 1899, though it began to function fully only in 1902, when it also received enlarged powers and responsibilities under the Education Act of that year. Finally, toward the end of the period the famous acts of early twentieth century Liberalism were passed. An Act of 1908 established old age pensions. The Labour Exchanges Act of 1909 set up a national system of employment exchanges, thus making comprehensive a device which had been started in some localities in 1902. And the National Insurance Act of 1911 introduced both health insurance and unemployment insurance, though much of the detailed administration of the health plan was left to the friendly societies, and trade unions were encouraged by subsidies to keep their own unemployment insurance schemes alive.[8] The general effect of these and other measures was to expand the various administrative departments and to create some new ones. As Table 3 suggests, the impact on the social service departments and on the "regulatory" agencies in the Trade, Industry, and Transport group was especially heavy. While the total military and civilian staff of the central government approximately doubled in size between 1891 and August 1914, the civilian employees of the government, including industrial workers, at least tripled (Table 2 and Table 4, Part A).

[8] Clapham, op. cit., Chap. VII.

The civilian agencies, however, were still small even at the end of the period.

If the general order of magnitude of these comparisons is correct, the growth of government in this first period was reflected in the considerable expansion of the armed forces, the multifold growth of defense workers in factories, and the doubling of the Post Office staff. Together, these categories probably accounted for five-sixths of the total growth. The regulatory and social service agencies of the government also grew rapidly, but they were of such minute size in 1890 that even their rapid expansion was of small consequence for the size of government as a whole.

On the eve of World War I, the British central government was still mainly a government of soldiers and sailors, postal clerks, and tax collectors. The only marked change over two generations was the sizable staff of industrial workers required in the government-owned armament establishments. But regulatory and social service activities still counted for little. By the broadest definition they absorbed not 10 per cent of the civilian employees of the central government and not more than 4 per cent of the military and civilian staffs together (Table 3 and Table 4, Part B).

FROM 1914 TO 1933

In the next twenty years, Britain was shaken by greater convulsions of war and economic distress than she had suffered for a century. By the time the seizure had begun to abate, her central government had changed, but, considering the circumstances, the change was surprisingly small (see Charts 3 and 4).

The crucial facts of the era were, first, the Great War; next, the economic problems involved in recovery and readjustment to postwar conditions; and, finally, the impact of the depression of 1929-1932. The central government expanded explosively in the course of World War I. Millions were mobilized into the armed forces. The civilian staff rose from nearly 325,000 in 1914 to over 850,000 in 1918 (Table 4, Part A). Of this increase of nearly 530,000 persons, about 390,000 were industrial workers, largely enlisted in the munitions factories and shipyards. Almost 100,000 more were officials, clerks, and other civilian employees in the defense ministries. These two categories together accounted for over 90 per cent of the wartime increase in the civilian staff.

Most of the remainder of the wartime increase came in two

TABLE 4

Central Government Employment, Selected Years, 1914-1950
A. Full-time Equivalent Workers[a]

Departmental Groups	Aug. 1, 1914	Nov. 2, 1918	April 1, 1928	April 1, 1933	April 1, 1936	April 1, 1939	April 1, 1945	April 1, 1950
Defense and supply	(469,252)	4,823,178	435,659	416,236	459,933	698,100	5,908,100	1,080,800
Armed forces	395,000	4,261,957	336,835	320,973	341,233	480,000	5,090,000	690,000
Non-industrial staff	7,252	105,721	21,415	21,452	27,000	52,400	239,900	122,800
Admiralty	4,366	16,882	7,684	7,316	8,600	12,900	54,400	30,800
War Office	1,636	18,539	9,453	9,507	10,800	19,800	67,500	33,500
Air Ministry	0	4,646	4,278	4,629	7,600	19,700	35,700	24,400
Min. of Supply	1,250	65,142	0	0	0	0	60,800	} 33,300
Min. of Aircraft Production	0	0	0	0	0	0	21,500	}
Other departments	0	512	0	0	0	0	0	800
Industrial staff	(67,000)	(455,500)	77,409	73,811	91,700	165,700	578,200	268,000
Admiralty	n.a.	n.a.	46,455	n.a.	51,000	71,600	154,800	97,800
War Office	n.a.	n.a.	24,253	n.a.	30,600	68,300	76,500	69,100
Air Ministry	n.a.	n.a.	6,701	n.a.	10,100	25,800	56,200	40,300
Min. of Supply	n.a.	n.a.	0	n.a.	0	0	290,700	60,800
Post Office	189,703	178,802	202,363	200,642	218,100	247,300	255,000	321,800
Non-industrial staff	171,848	158,676	169,056	171,277	182,200	196,200	208,500	249,900
Industrial staff	17,855	20,126	33,307	29,365	35,900	51,100	46,500	71,900
Revenue departments (non-industrial)	20,009	21,182	29,376	33,517	36,800	40,000	46,900	64,000
Inland Revenue	9,753	10,958	17,944	20,835	22,800	25,000	37,500	49,800
Customs and Excise	10,256	10,224	11,432	12,682	14,000	15,000	9,400	14,200
Social service (non-industrial)	8,109	15,221	18,100	15,446	21,900	24,800	37,700	73,900
Min. of Education	3,309	2,445	3,185	3,121	1,800	2,100	1,500	3,300
Min. of Health	0	0	6,412	6,791	5,900	6,700	3,600	5,900

(continued on next page)

TABLE 4, PART A (continued)

Departmental Groups	Aug. 1, 1914	Nov. 2, 1918	April 1, 1928	April 1, 1933	April 1, 1936	April 1, 1939	April 1, 1945	April 1, 1950
Min. of Housing and Local Government	1,045	921	0	0	0	0	500	1,300
Min. of Pensions	0	8,561	7,213	3,896	3,200	3,000	11,300	11,000
National Assistance Board	0	0	0	0	6,600	8,100	8,700	8,500
Min. of National Insurance	3,443	3,058	0	0	0	0	5,600	35,500
Central Land Bd. and War Damage Comm.	0	0	0	0	0	0	2,200	3,100
Other departments	312	236	1,290	1,638	4,400	4,900	4,300	5,300
Trade, industry, and transport	n.a.	n.a.	27,088	n.a.	39,900	48,100	115,600	128,000
Non-industrial staff	11,085	49,955	23,420	34,489	34,800	42,900	110,900	113,700
Min. of Agriculture and Fisheries	3,381	3,903	2,302	2,450	1,700	2,700	3,700	16,800
Forestry Commission	95	103	n.a.	n.a.	n.a.	500	500	2,000
Board of Trade	2,535	7,036	4,607	4,191	4,300	4,800	6,800	10,100
Min. of Food	0	9,181	0	0	0	0	37,900	30,800
Min. of Transport	0	0	0	0	} 2,200	} 3,000	14,900	6,900
Min. of Shipping	0	2,690	n.a.	} n.a.				
Min. of Fuel and Power	0	0	0	0	0	0	6,900	} 6,400
Mines Department	0	0	0	0	400	500	6,600	
Min. of Civil Aviation	0	0	0	0	0	0	0	5,300
Dept. of Scientific and Industrial Research	0	605	n.a.	n.a.	1,300	1,500	1,900	2,900
Min. of Labour	4,428	8,484	13,529	23,897	} 23,300	} 28,300	35,600	29,900
Min. of National Service	0	15,124	0	0				
Other departments	646	2,829	2,982	3,951	1,600	1,600	3,000	2,600
Industrial staff								
Forestry Commission	n.a.	n.a.	3,668	n.a.	5,100	5,200	4,700	14,300
Min. of Transport	n.a.	n.a.	3,450	n.a.	4,000	5,200	4,700	12,100
Min. of Civil Aviation	n.a.	n.a.	218	n.a.	1,100	n.a.	0	2,200

(continued on next page)

TABLE 4, PART A (continued)

Departmental Groups	Aug. 1, 1914	Nov. 2, 1918	April 1, 1928	April 1, 1933	April 1, 1936	April 1, 1939	April 1, 1945	April 1, 1950
Agency services								
Non-industrial staff	1,548	4,447	3,884	4,012	5,700	10,400	21,600	26,900
Ordnance survey	0	0	n.a.	n.a.	1,400	2,500	1,900	4,600
Stationery Office	517	2,627	n.a.	n.a.	1,100	1,600	2,600	3,200
Min. of Works	719	1,239	n.a.	n.a.	3,200	6,300	14,300	17,600
Mint	277	432	n.a.	n.a.	0	0	0	0
Other departments	35	149	n.a.	n.a.	0	0	2,800	1,500
(Agency services, total)	n.a.	n.a.	9,816	n.a.	13,500	20,000	46,100	59,800
Industrial staff	n.a.	n.a.	5,932	n.a.	7,800	9,600	24,500	32,900
Stationery Office	n.a.	n.a.	2,157	n.a.	2,300	3,000	4,100	4,400
Min. of Works	n.a.	n.a.	3,776	n.a.	5,500	6,600	20,400	28,500
Central government, home and legal departments (non-industrial)	8,253	9,194	11,861	12,969	14,200	17,900	29,300	23,500
Central Govt. and Finance	1,010	2,060	2,283	2,452	n.a.	n.a.	n.a.	n.a.
Home office	3,259	3,486	}	}	1,100	2,500	5,800	4,000
Legal departments	} 3,984	2,802	} 9,578	} 10,517	n.a.	n.a.	n.a.	n.a.
Prison Commission	}	846	}	}	3,400	3,600	3,100	5,400
Min. of Information	0	0	0	0	n.a.	n.a.	n.a.	n.a.
Postal and Tel. Censorship Dept.	0	0	n.a. (in 9,578)	n.a. (in 10,517)	0	0	9,500	0
Other departments	0	0	0	0	9,700	11,800	10,900	14,100
Foreign and imperial services (non-industrial)	955	2,309	2,386	1,979	2,600	2,800	9,800	10,100
Foreign Office	187	835	n.a.	n.a.	1,600	1,700	6,800	6,200
Colonial Office	214	240	n.a.	n.a.	n.a.	n.a.	n.a.	n.a.
India Office	544	744	n.a.	n.a.	n.a.	n.a.	n.a.	n.a.
Other departments	0	490	n.a.	n.a.	1,000	1,100	3,000	3,900
Misc. industrial staffs	(10,000)[b]	(10,000)[b]	4,478	13,924[b]	4,400	8,600	11,200	9,800

Note: For 1928 and 1933 the figures for Home office, Legal departments, and Prison Commission are combined (braced) into a single figure (9,578 and 10,517 respectively); for 1914 the figures for Legal departments and Prison Commission are combined (3,984).

(continued on next page)

TABLE 4, PART A (continued)

Departmental Groups	Aug. 1, 1914	Nov. 2, 1918	April 1, 1928	April 1, 1933	April 1, 1936	April 1, 1939	April 1, 1945	April 1, 1950
Summary								
Defense and supply	(469,252)	(4,823,178)	435,659	416,236	459,933	698,100	5,908,100	1,080,800
Armed forces	395,000	4,261,957	336,835	320,973	341,233	480,000	5,090,000	690,000
Non-industrial defense staff	7,252	105,721	21,415	21,452	27,000	52,400	239,900	122,800
Industrial defense staff	(67,000)	(455,500)	77,409	73,811	91,700	165,700	578,200	268,000
Civilian agencies	(249,662)	(291,110)	310,472	321,961	355,400	409,500	551,600	690,900
Non-industrial staff	221,807	260,984	263,087	278,672	302,200	335,000	464,700	562,000
Industrial staff	(27,855)	(30,126)	47,385	43,289	53,200	74,500	86,900	128,900
Total	(718,914)	(5,114,288)	746,131c	738,197c	815,333c	1,107,600	6,459,700	1,771,700

[a] Part-time workers counted one-half with exceptions described in Appendix, "Sources and Notes to Tables and Charts."
[b] Includes all industrial staff other than Defense and Post Office.
[c] Includes staffs of reserved and agency services in Northern Ireland as follows: 1928, 5,004; 1933, 4,983; 1936, 4,000. In later years, these staffs are distributed by department.
Note: Figures in parentheses represent estimates.
n.a. = not available.

TABLE 4 (continued)

Central Government Employment, Selected Years, 1914-1950

B. Departmental Staffs as a Percentage of Total Central Government Employment

Departmental Groups	Aug. 1, 1914	Nov. 2, 1918	April 1, 1928	April 1, 1933	April 1, 1936	April 1, 1939	April 1, 1945	April 1, 1950
Defense and supply	65.3	94.3	58.4	56.4	56.4	63.0	91.5	61.0
Armed forces	54.9	83.3	45.1	43.5	41.9	43.3	78.8	38.9
Non-industrial staff	1.0	2.1	2.9	2.9	3.3	4.7	3.7	6.9
Industrial staff	9.3	8.9	10.4	10.0	11.2	15.0	9.0	15.1
Post Office	26.4	3.5	27.1	27.2	26.7	22.3	3.9	18.2
Non-industrial staff	23.9	3.1	22.6	23.2	22.3	17.7	3.2	14.1
Industrial staff	2.5	0.4	4.5	4.0	4.4	4.6	0.7	4.1
Revenue departments	2.8	0.4	3.9	4.5	4.5	3.6	0.7	3.6
Social services	1.1	0.3	2.4	2.1	2.7	2.2	0.6	4.2
Trade, indus., and transport	n.a.	n.a.	3.6	n.a.	4.9	4.3	1.8	7.2
Non-industrial staff	1.5	1.0	3.1	4.7	4.3	3.9	1.7	6.4
Industrial staff	n.a.	n.a.	0.5	n.a.	0.6	0.4	0.1	0.8
Agency services	n.a.	n.a.	1.3	n.a.	1.7	1.8	0.7	3.4
Non-industrial staff	0.2	0.1	0.5	0.5	0.7	0.9	0.3	1.5
Industrial staff	n.a.	n.a.	0.8	n.a.	1.0	0.9	0.4	1.9
Central govt., home and legal dept.	1.1	0.2	1.6	1.8	1.7	1.6	0.5	1.3
Foreign and imperial services	0.1	0.05	0.3	0.3	0.3	0.3	0.15	0.6
Misc. industrial staffs	1.4	0.2	0.6	1.9	0.5	0.8	0.2	0.6
Summary								
Defense and supply	65.3	94.3	58.4	56.4	56.4	63.0	91.5	61.0
Armed forces	54.9	83.3	45.1	43.5	41.9	43.3	78.8	38.9
Non-industrial defense staff	1.0	2.1	2.9	2.9	3.3	4.7	3.7	6.9
Industrial defense staff	9.3	8.9	10.4	10.0	11.2	15.0	9.0	15.1
Civilian agencies	34.7	5.7	41.6	43.6	43.6	37.0	8.5	39.0
Non-industrial staff	30.8	5.1	35.3	37.7	37.1	30.2	7.2	31.7
Industrial staff	3.9	0.6	6.3	5.9	6.5	6.7	1.3	7.3
Total[a]	100.0	100.0	100.0	100.0	100.0	100.0	100.0	100.0

[a] Includes staffs of reserved and agency services in Northern Ireland as follows: 1928, 0.7 per cent; 1933, 0.7 per cent; 1936,

TABLE 4 (continued)

Central Government Employment, Selected Years, 1914-1950

C. Departmental Staffs as a Percentage of Total Working Population

Departmental Groups	Aug. 1, 1914	Nov. 2, 1918	April 1, 1928	April 1, 1933	April 1, 1936	April 1, 1939	April 1, 1945	April 1, 1950
Defense and supply	2.46	24.39	2.10	1.93	2.07	3.05	24.38	4.69
Armed forces	2.07	21.55	1.62	1.49	1.54	2.09	21.00	2.99
Non-industrial staff	0.04	0.53	0.10	0.10	0.12	0.23	0.99	0.53
Industrial staff	0.35	2.30	0.37	0.34	0.41	0.72	2.39	1.16
Post Office								
Non-industrial staff	0.99	0.90	0.97	0.93	0.98	1.08	1.05	1.39
Industrial staff	0.90	0.80	0.81	0.79	0.82	0.86	0.86	1.08
Revenue departments	0.09	0.10	0.16	0.14	0.16	0.22	0.19	0.31
Social services	0.10	0.11	0.14	0.16	0.17	0.17	0.19	0.28
Trade, industry, and transport								
Non-industrial staff	n.a.	n.a.	0.13	n.a.	0.18	0.21	0.48	0.55
Industrial staff	0.06	0.25	0.11	0.16	0.16	0.19	0.46	0.49
Agency services								
Non-industrial staff	n.a.	n.a.	0.05	n.a.	0.06	0.09	0.19	0.26
Industrial staff	0.01	0.02	0.02	0.02	0.03	0.05	0.09	0.12
Central govt., home, and legal depts.	0.04	0.05	0.06	0.06	0.06	0.08	0.12	0.10
Foreign and imperial services	0.005	0.01	0.01	0.01	0.01	0.01	0.04	0.10
Misc. industrial staffs	0.05	0.05	0.02	0.06	0.02	0.04	0.05	0.04
Summary								
Defense and supply	2.46	24.39	2.10	1.93	2.07	3.05	24.38	4.69
Armed forces	2.07	21.55	1.62	1.49	1.54	2.09	21.00	2.99
Non-industrial defense staff	0.04	0.53	0.10	0.10	0.12	0.23	0.99	0.53
Industrial defense staff	0.35	2.30	0.37	0.34	0.41	0.72	2.39	1.16
Civilian agencies	1.31	1.47	1.49	1.49	1.60	1.79	2.27	3.00
Non-industrial staff	1.16	1.32	1.27	1.29	1.36	1.46	1.92	2.44
Industrial staff	0.15	0.15	0.23	0.20	0.24	0.33	0.36	0.56
Total	3.77	25.86	3.59	3.42	3.67	4.83	26.65	7.68

CHART 3

Number of Civilian Central Government Workers Employed in Various Functions, Selected Years, 1914-1950

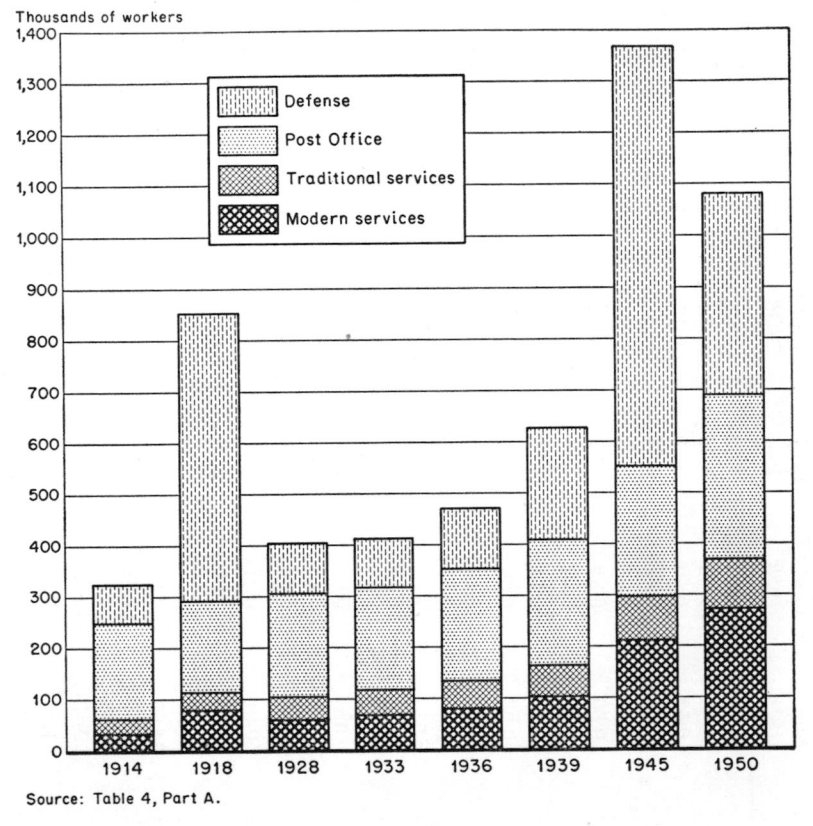

Source: Table 4, Part A.

categories: the group of economic regulatory agencies which the British Treasury refers to as Trade, Industry, and Transport; and the social service sphere. Before the war the regulatory group consisted mainly of the Boards of Trade and of Agriculture and Fisheries. In the course of the war, there was not only a considerable extension of the regulatory work of these departments, but there were established ministries for Food, for Shipping, for Mines, for Blockade, and for Reconstruction, as well as departments for Overseas Trade and for Scientific and Industrial Research. In addition, a Ministry of Labour was created which absorbed the Board of Trade's responsibilities for employment exchanges, unemployment insurance, and labor market

CHART 4

Percentage Distribution of Civilian Central Government
Workers among Main Functional Divisions, Selected Years,
1914-1950

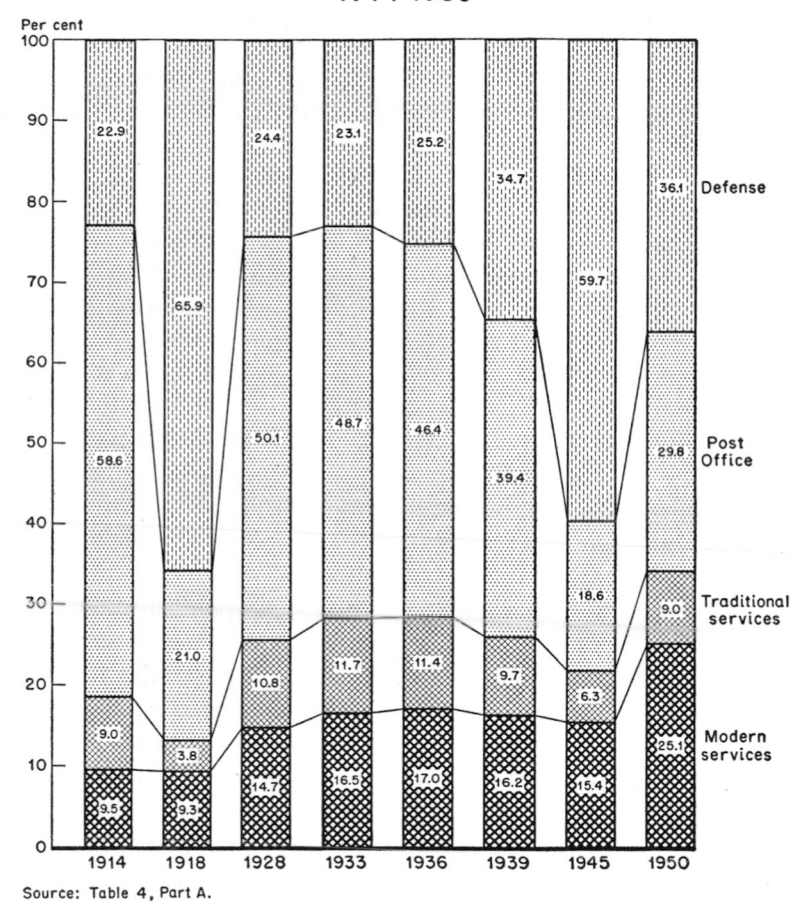

Source: Table 4, Part A.

information, and a Ministry of National Service was established
to supervise the withdrawal of labor for the armed forces. Regulation of economic life became a most important government
function during the war. The personnel engaged rose from
11,000 to nearly 50,000.

In the social service sphere the need to provide compensation
for those injured in the war and for the families of those killed
brought about the creation of a Ministry of Pensions, whose staff
included more than 8,500 persons at the end of the war.

With the end of the fighting, a number of conditions, some permissive and some compelling, combined to bring about the virtual dismantling of the wartime structure. Substantial demobilization of the defense establishment was inevitable in view of the prime fact that the defeat of the Central Powers removed all immediate danger of serious international conflict. Additional pressure was provided by the provisions of the Treaty of Versailles, by the popular view that armaments were in themselves a cause of war, and by the activities of the League of Nations. All this was supported by a complex of domestic factors which favored budgetary economy, not only in the military sphere, but in government at large.

In the world of politics, the 1920's were the years of the decline of the Liberal Party. Taken together with the country's distrust of the still-untried Labour politicians, the result was a long period of Tory dominance in Parliament which made for restraint in government activity. The Labour Party did, indeed, twice form governments (1924 and 1929-1931). On both occasions, however, the Labourites depended on Liberal support, and, as it happened, Philip Snowden, their Chancellor of the Exchequer, proved just as orthodox in finance as were his Conservative counterparts.

In Britain's postwar situation, financial and political orthodoxy meant economy. It did so in part because of a Conservative yearning, backed by the temper of a large part of the country, to restore, so far as possible, the conditions of pre-war days, and in part because of a desire for lower taxes. In addition, economy was a necessary counterpart to the restoration and maintenance of the gold standard at the old par of exchange, on which financiers and many economists relied to regain for Britain her old position in finance and trade. When the Great Depression came, economy emerged again as the orthodox reaction to losses of tax revenue and foreign exchange. Economy, however, was not a policy which could be consistently pursued. Persistent demands for governmental aid for housing, education, and most of all for unemployment relief, backed, as they were, by votes, were met at least in part, though with restraint and sometimes at the expense of still more far-reaching savings in other spheres.

By 1933 the war-swollen employment rolls of the central government had been reduced to their 1914 level. The government's share in the labor force fell from 3.8 to 3.4 per cent (Table 4, Part C) chiefly as a result of a decline in manpower used for defense. The drive for economy left its mark on the civilian departments as evidenced by the small net increase in those branches. This increase was only some 29 per cent, compared with over 100 per cent both in the 1890-1914 period and in the period since 1933. The divergent movements, or lack of movement, in the chief departments of government are summarized in Table 5.

TABLE 5

Changes in Central Government Employment between
August 1914 and April 1933

	Thousands of Persons	Per Cent
Defense	−53.0	−11.3
Post Office	+10.9	+5.8
Traditional services	+19.2	+65.9
Revenue	+13.5	+67.5
Central govt., home and legal depts.	+4.7	+57.1
Foreign and imperial	+1.0	+107.2
Modern services	+37.1	+120.8
Social services	+7.3	+90.5
Trade, industry, transport[a]	+23.4	+211.1
Ministry of Labour	+19.5	+439.7
Economic regulatory agencies	+3.9	+59.1
Agency services[a]	+2.5	+159.2
Industrial staffs	+3.9	+39.0
Total	+19.3	+2.7

[a] Non-industrial staff only.

In part, the very moderate rate of increase in the civilian departments is accounted for by the trend of Post Office business, which was not much larger in 1933 than in 1914.[9] And this, together with some improvement in productivity, confined the growth of employment in this huge department to less than 6 per cent.

In other branches, increases were more substantial. Growth

[9] For example, the number of letters, newspapers, etc., carried rose only 15 per cent, the number of parcels, 11 per cent. An increase in local telephone messages of 36 per cent was offset, in part, by a decline in inland telegraph messages of 47 per cent.

in the revenue-collecting agencies resulted from: the larger collection and the larger number of taxpayers; the higher tax rates, which made taxpayers more energetic in protecting their rights and so increased the volume of disputed cases; the greater complexity of the laws; and the greater variety of tax laws to be administered.[10] There was also an increase in the agencies dealing with law and justice.

Still larger increases occurred in the group identified in Table 5 as the "modern" services of government. Total employment in the group more than doubled, but the major changes centered in the social service area and in the Ministry of Labour. The latter department, the staff of which administered the expanding scheme of unemployment insurance and various schemes for retraining the unemployed and increasing their mobility, and which provided labor market information on a more elaborate scale, quintupled in size. The Ministry of Housing and Local Government was transformed into the Ministry of Health. It became responsible for the supervision of the ever more ramified work of the local authorities, particularly in the field of public health (see Chapter 5), and for the administration of several new acts to encourage slum clearance and house building. Its staff increased to over six times its 1914 size. Between them the Labour and Health ministries accounted for an increase of more than 25,000 out of some 37,000 workers in the group of modern services.

Apart from the staff of the Ministry of Health, the growth of employment in the Social Service group was slow over the period as a whole. The same was true of the economic regulatory agencies. In the attempt to eliminate government intervention in industry and trade, all the major wartime economic agencies were abolished and the activities of the Ministry of Agriculture were severely cut. The Board of Trade remained larger than before the war, but only some 60 per cent as large as it was when peace returned.

We may conclude, then, that in spite of a great wartime upheaval, and apart from certain special branches of activity, the growth of central government was substantially checked during 1914-1933.

[10] Cf. *Third Report of Committee on National Expenditure*, 1922, Cmd. 1589, p. 33.

SINCE 1933

The circumstances which produced this check were, however, short-lived. With the advent of Hitler and the war that followed, the country was once more rearmed, and the elaborate machinery of government economic activity and regulation was rebuilt and extended. After World War II, the military services were demobilized only incompletely. The demobilization of economic controls was, in the end, quite extensive; but it was longer delayed than after World War I, left a persistent residue of intervention, and embodied a wide extension of the social services. Over the whole period 1933-1950, employment by the central government rose from something over 700,000 to nearly 1,800,000, expanding its share of the labor force from 3.4 to 7.7 per cent (Table 4, Parts A and C).

Although, in general, this study follows the history of public employment only through 1950, the fairly important change in circumstances and in public policy since the return to power of a Conservative Government in 1951 requires at least brief notice of more recent events. Between 1950 and 1955, rearmament pushed defense employment to higher levels. Over the same period, civilian employment declined as many economic controls were eased or abandoned. The net result was an increase in the total numbers employed by central government, which raised its share of the labor force virtually to 8 per cent. Employment for defense purposes in April 1955 was three times larger than in 1933; that for civilian purposes had approximately doubled. Table 6 summarizes the main directions of change.

The pace of military activity began to pick up as early as 1936. By the end of the war, over 5,000,000 persons were in the armed forces, 240,000 were engaged in non-industrial work for the defense departments, and 578,000 were employed in munitions factories and other industrial works owned by the government. This wartime increase closely parallels that in World War I, but what happened to it after the end of the second war was markedly different. In the 1920's the defeat of Germany had provided a temporary respite from the threat of conflict among the major powers. The armed forces had been quickly reduced to pre-war size and then below. After World War II, on the other hand, the quarrel between Russia and the West first prevented so large a demobilization and then required a considerable rearmament effort begin-

TABLE 6

Changes in Central Government Employment,
April 1933 to April 1955

| | CHANGE BETWEEN SPECIFIED YEARS | | | | | |
| | 1933-1950 | | 1950-1955 | | 1933-1955 | |
	Thousands of Persons	Per Cent	Thousands of Persons	Per Cent	Thousands of Persons	Per Cent
Defense	+664.6	+159.7	+193.2	+17.9	+857.8	+206.1
Armed forces	+369.0	+115.0	+149.0	+21.6	+518.0	+161.4
Civilian staffs	+295.5	+310.2	+44.2	+11.3	+339.7	+356.6
Post Office	+121.2	+60.4	+4.1	+1.3	+125.3	+62.4
Traditional services	+49.1	+101.4	+0.1	+0.1	+49.2	+101.5
Revenue	+30.5	+90.9	+1.4	+2.2	+31.9	+95.2
Central govt., home and legal depts.	+10.5	+81.2	+0.4	+1.7	+10.9	+84.0
Foreign and imperial	+8.1	+410.4	-1.7	-16.8	+6.4	+323.4
Modern services	+203.6	+300.0	-69.5	-25.6	+134.1	+197.6
Social services	+58.5	+378.4	-8.0	-10.8	+50.5	+326.9
Trade, industry, and transport[a]	+79.2	+229.7	-44.6	-39.2	+34.6	+100.3
Ministry of Labour	+6.0	+25.1	-7.0	-23.4	-1.0	-4.2
Economic regulatory agencies	+73.2	+691.2	-37.6	-44.9	+35.6	+336.1
Agency services[a]	+22.9	+570.5	-6.1	-22.7	+16.8	+418.7
Industrial staffs	+43.1	+309.4	-10.8	-18.9	+32.3	+232.0
Total	+1,033.5	+140.0	+127.9	+7.2	+1,161.4	+157.3

[a] Non-industrial staff only.

ning after the outbreak of war in Korea. By 1955, the armed forces stood at two and one-half times their pre-war strength. Moreover, the great development of mechanization caused a sharp increase in civilian defense staffs. The non-industrial defense staff in 1955 was five times its 1936 size, and the industrial staff had more than tripled.

When recovery from depression reduced the pressure for economy, the civilian agencies began to grow. By 1939 nearly 90,000 additional persons had been hired. Half of these were in the Post Office, where activity was stimulated by improving business. Protracted unemployment had earlier caused the government to create an Unemployment Assistance Board to administer relief outside the insurance scheme. This move, designed partly to relieve the local authorities and partly to reduce the expense of the dole, involved a staff of 8,000. The institution of a general tariff, as well as higher taxes, helped push employment in the revenue departments up by 6,500. For the rest, a variety of moves were made to subsidize or to cartelize industry and agriculture and to extend social legislation.[11] Among them were the establishment of statutory cartels in a number of industries, special schemes to encourage investment in depressed areas and to transfer workers out, and a small beginning of town and country planning.

During World War II the civilian agencies grew even more rapidly. Although the increase in activity was largely confined to functions engendered by the war itself, these were so varied that every important group of agencies grew rapidly. Burdened by the administration of war pensions and war damage claims, the social service group grew by some 50 per cent from 1939 to 1945. Booming construction needs caused the Ministry of Works, which is responsible for the construction and housekeeping needs of government departments and for administering certain controls over building materials and the construction industry, to increase by 130 per cent. The Home and Legal Departments grew by two-thirds. But the most dramatic increases took place in the departments regulating trade, industry, and transport. Ministries of Food, Production, Economic Warfare, and Reconstruction were established; the Department of Mines grew into the Ministry of Fuel and Power; the Ministry of Transport ab-

[11] Cf. P. J. D. Wiles, "Pre-War and War-Time Controls," in *The British Economy, 1945-50*, G. D. N. Worswick and P. H. Ady, editors, Oxford, 1952.

sorbed the shipping department of the Board of Trade and was transformed into the Ministry of War Transport.

In addition to monetary measures to control inflation, the government undertook to regulate investment directly; it controlled foreign exchange and forbade foreign issues; it engaged in direct purchase of imports, of essential raw materials, and of foods. Prices were fixed, consumer and producer goods were rationed, and some trades were subsidized. Wages were influenced through compulsory arbitration; workers were not only conscripted for the armed forces, but their right to shift among civilian jobs was limited, and there was positive direction of labor to essential jobs. The work of some industries whose output was limited was concentrated in one or a few firms. The use of many materials was limited to specified purposes; the production of many commodities was forbidden or directly controlled with respect to quantity, quality, or packaging, while the output of other commodities, notably farm products and coal, was pushed. Employment in the regulatory agencies[12] quadrupled during the war, a rate of growth rivaled only by the service ministries themselves. All in all, some 145,000 additional employees were hired by the civilian agencies between 1939 and 1945.

Afterward the development of the civilian departments followed a checkered course. With the return of peace, the social services were widely extended. Government building and repairs required an increase of labor in the agency services. At the same time, the Labour Government undertook generally to maintain many of the economic controls established during the war. By 1950, employment had increased 25 per cent in the civilian agencies other than the Post Office. Since the Conservatives regained power in 1951, however, there has been a marked abandonment or relaxation of controls. The staffs of the economic regulatory agencies were severely cut, and the activities of the agency services were also sharply curtailed. Employment in the group of Modern Services, as a whole, has fallen by fully one-quarter.

The net outcome has been that the civilian agencies other than the Post Office have grown during World War II and its aftermath in a degree very like that in World War I and its aftermath. During both wars, employment in these agencies increased some-

[12] Exclusive of the Ministry of Labour, which combined regulatory and social service functions.

what over 80 per cent.[13] Ten years after World War I, employment stood some 8 per cent below its level at the war's end. Ten years after World War II, employment, despite an interim rise, was back to its war-end level.[14]

This general similarity, however, conceals very significant differences. In the first place, as already stated, the cutback in staff after World War I began more promptly. More important, a large part of the increase in the modern services after World War I took place in the Ministry of Labour and reflected the need to deal with that period's chronic and depression-born unemployment. Another considerable part was in the Ministry of Health and was associated with a great increase in local government activity. In the 1939-1955 period, on the other hand, Ministry of Labour personnel declined nearly 20 per cent. The economic regulatory agencies proper increased their staffs by 32,000 persons or 220 per cent in that period (between 1933 and 1955, by 336 per cent). This compares with an increase of only 3,200

[13] Post Office employment measured by our figures declined 6 per cent during World War I, then increased 13 per cent from 1918 to 1928. During World War II it increased 3 per cent, and another 26 per cent from 1945 to 1950.

[14] Considering that the periods are of somewhat different length, the rates of growth are, in fact, almost exactly the same. Indeed, if one makes allowances for the wartime bulges, the rate of growth in this sector as a whole has been notably steady since 1914, when it can first be separately distinguished. The following figures are revealing.

| | | INDEXES FOR CIVIL CENTRAL GOVERNMENT EMPLOYMENT, EXCLUDING POST OFFICE | |
PERIOD	DURATION (years)	Actual Indexes	Indexes for Growth Rate of 4% per Annum
World War I and 10 post-war years	14	1914=100	100
		1928=172	173
Inter-war period	11	1928=100	100
		1939=157	154
World War II and 10 post-war years	16	1939=100	100
		1955=185	187
War and peace	41	1914=100	100
		1955=500	499

The present writers are not the discoverers of this striking regularity. It was first observed and described by that remarkable anonymous student of government whose single brilliant memoir announced Parkinson's Law (*Economist*, November 19, 1955).

55

persons, or 48 per cent between 1914 and 1928. The more recent period has thus been marked by a far more rapid growth of staff devoted to economic controls.

In a similar way, in 1955 the staffs of the social service agencies as a whole were over 40,000, or 165 per cent, higher than in 1939, and 50,000, or 327 per cent, higher than in 1933. By contrast the rise from 1914 to 1928 was only 10,000, or 123 per cent. The growth of staff in the later period was clearly more rapid than in the earlier. Moreover, the more recent decades reflect primarily an expansion of the work of the central government itself, rather than the encouragement and supervision of local activity.

The causes of the growth since the early thirties and of the directions it has taken are to be found partly in tendencies which have been growing in strength for many decades and partly in certain factors peculiar to World War II and to the period thereafter. Among the persistent forces was the continued shift of effective political power to the lower income groups. In the inter-war period, traditional political allegiances were in a state of flux and dominant power remained with the Conservatives. The Labour Party, however, continued to attract voters from both the working class and the middle class. Its significant, although not steady, growth was aided by the split among the Liberals, by the failure of orthodox economic policy to cope successfully with the depression, and later by the Conservatives' association with Munich. By the end of the 1930's, therefore, the Labour Party had emerged as a far more powerful instrument for expressing the aspirations of the working classes.

These aspirations are by no means confined to Labour supporters, but they are most strongly expressed in that party's programs. They may be stated categorically as follows: (1) the attainment and protection of "national minima" of income, health care, housing, and education; (2) the control and reduction of the major risks of industrial capitalism, chiefly business cycles, industrial hazards, and urban health dangers; (3) a more nearly equal sharing, not only of income, but of industrial authority; and (4) the deliberate state control of resources to promote the common good, as a substitute for reliance upon the market.

Acceptance of these goals had been spreading among the British people for a long time, and the triumph of certain new views on economics associated with the name of Lord Keynes considerably increased their influence. These doctrines appeared, on the one hand, to demonstrate that it was within the power of government to avoid at least major depressions, and, on the other hand, to remove one of the great checks to the transfer of income to the poor, namely, the fear that such transfers might seriously impede the accumulation of capital. After the appearance of Keynes' *General Theory of Employment, Interest and Money* in 1936, a broad section of the Labour program gained the support of professional economic opinion to a degree it had not had before.

Responding to the clear drift of public opinion, the wartime government took several steps. Its notable White Paper on Full Employment[15] laid down a general program for the stabilization of employment for later years. In addition, the government appointed a number of committees of investigation. Their reports on housing, on urban and country planning, and on industrial location, for example, looked toward a far greater degree of government intervention when peace returned. The most influential document was the Beveridge report on *Social Insurance and the Allied Services*. This and Beveridge's non-official book *Full Employment in a Free Society* added the weight of official statistics and analysis and the prestige of an outstanding former civil servant to the more general programs of the politicians. Beveridge's analysis won such a wide measure of public support that it became clear that any post-war government would go a considerable distance to implement his recommendations. Nevertheless, the defeat of the Conservatives in 1945 may be attributed in part to public fear that that party would not go far enough.

The persistent forces, of which these political and ideological developments were expressions, were bolstered by the experiences of the war and the problems of the post-war period. World War I had already demonstrated the feasibility, if not the complete success, of government regulation of resource allocation, of production, and of distribution. World War II, with its more nearly total mobilization of resources, was a demonstration on a grander scale. It was generally felt that the more extensive intervention in the second war organized the productive power of the country more effectively and distributed the burdens of the war more equitably than had been done a generation earlier.

[15] *Employment Policy*, Ministry of Reconstruction, 1944, Cmd. 6527.

However vexatious in their intimate application, controls which, in their broader aspects, seemed to work so effectively for the workers' benefit during the war were not to be lightly abandoned by them or by the party which aimed to represent them. This reluctance to return to the market was aggravated when it became clear that—in the face of the depletion of Britain's foreign investment, the disruption of her export trade, and the drain of continuing defense expenditures—the extended social services would be a severe economic strain in the first years of peace. In this situation, even the wartime Coalition Government was prepared to maintain many of the economic controls which had earlier been viewed only as wartime expedients. The Labour Government, when it took over, supported them with enthusiasm. They were relaxed only gradually so long as that party remained in power. Under the Conservative Government, most wartime and post-war controls have, indeed, been abandoned. There remains, however, a significant residue, and this seems to represent an expansion in the economic role of the state capable of enduring even under a government generally antipathetic to intervention, and even after many of the immediate difficulties of the post-war period had been overcome.

In the complex adjustment of the civilian agencies to their peacetime functions, three lines of development stand out. In the first place, certain departments furnishing only indirect support for the war effort had been starved of manpower during the conflict itself, sometimes in the face of large additional burdens. When labor became more plentiful after the war, these departments quickly expanded. The revenue departments and the Post Office are prominent examples of these conditions, although, presumably, they applied generally. Government revenues increased three and one-half times between 1939 and 1945, but the personnel of the tax-collecting agencies rose only some 17 per cent. There was therefore a large increase after the war both to relieve the strain on the staff and to handle the further expansion of receipts between 1945 and 1950. Post Office personnel also increased markedly after 1945, although in this case there is no clear indication of a substantial increase in the volume of business during the war. The need to enlarge the staff in these departments was all the greater because hours of work were reduced after the war's end.[16]

[16] See Chapter 7, note 3.

The second line of development after World War II has been the very large expansion of the social services. Foreshadowed by the comprehensive Beveridge report, action was taken on many fronts after the war. The National Health Service Act of 1946 provided for free medical care for the entire population. Its central administration was made the chief responsibility of the Ministry of Health, whose responsibilities for local government were transferred to a new Ministry of Housing and Local Government. The National Insurance Act consolidated and strengthened existing arrangements covering the risks of unemployment, old age, and ill health. It was supplemented by a new act covering industrial injuries and by the establishment of a system of family allowances. Administration was centralized in a new Ministry of National Insurance, which in 1955, after consolidating with the Ministry of Pensions, had nearly 38,000 employees. A National Assistance Act provided a new central system for relief of poverty. The Education Act of 1944 laid the basis for a national system of secondary education, and while administration remained largely a local burden, larger powers of decision were given to a newly established Ministry of Education. The Housing Acts of 1946 and 1949 extended the subsidies offered for new home building and involved a larger volume of central administration. Taken as a group, the social service departments nearly doubled their staffs between 1945 and 1950 and nearly tripled them between 1939 and 1950.

The third line of adjustment has had to do with the administration of controls over labor, production, and markets. Because of the change in policies which followed the shift of governments in 1951, the transition to peacetime conditions has been less straightforward in this sector. A brief résumé will suggest the main changes between the end of the war and today.[17]

Fairly comprehensive controls over manpower had been set up during the war to prevent men in certain occupations from changing jobs without government permission, to prevent firms from hiring workers except through the official employment exchanges, and in some cases to direct workers to particular industries by persuasion or order. In general, these controls were quickly abandoned after the war. For some years, indeed, they were maintained

[17] Cf. Worswick and Ady, *op.cit.*; also Central Office of Information, *Britain, An Official Handbook*, London, H.M.S.O., 1956, Chaps. V, VII, IX, and XI, and British Information Service, *Labor and Industry in Britain*, various issues.

for coal mining and agriculture and at times for other industries. They are now completely abandoned, with the exception that employers in most industries must report their vacancies to official employment exchanges and engage their workers only through these agencies.

Controls over imports were retained for some years with full wartime rigor. For a time also the government remained the sole purchaser of the major imported raw materials and foodstuffs. Allocations systems for raw materials, however, were gradually abandoned as supplies increased. There has also been a gradual changeover from state to private trading in imported goods, which began under the Labour Government and has been completed under the Conservatives. Control over private purchases abroad has been considerably relaxed, although licensing is still used to restrict the quantity of many imports and the source of many more. There is a residue of export controls, now chiefly confined to goods of strategic importance. Exchange control, moreover, remains in force, although there has been some relaxation in its operation.

Building construction remained under strict licensing control for some years after the war, but restrictions began to be relaxed in 1953, and licensing was abolished in 1954. Construction, however, is not free of government control. It is influenced through a continuing system of subsidies to local authorities for house construction and slum clearance, through the government's supervision of the borrowing programs of local authorities, and through the government's powers over the location of industry (see below). In addition, not only building construction but investment at large is subject to the government's influence on interest rates and to its control over finance exercised through the Capital Issues Committee. Some of these controls represent activities established or greatly enlarged since the war.

Rationing and price control of consumer goods, widely maintained in the early post-war years, have been gradually abolished. The prices of bread, milk, and potatoes, however, continue to be fixed, and the great majority of houses let are still subject to rent control.

It is important to remember that although formal controls over most commodities, both consumer and producer goods, have been dropped, the government continues to maintain a close watch over supply and output, to collect industrial statistics for purposes of record and possible future regulatory needs, and to influence the course of events by consultation with industry. In general, each industry in the country remains connected with the government through a specified ministry which acts as the industry's "production department." The production departments not only perform statutory functions with regard to the industry they watch, but attempt to be versed in its problems and to sponsor its interests within the government. They encourage the establishment of joint councils of employers and workers, give technical advice, and in other ways try to promote efficiency in industry.

In still other directions, the scope of wartime regulation was maintained or even extended. Agriculture is an outstanding example. The war had already seen something like a 25 per cent increase in agricultural output as a result of government-proffered market incentives and government direction. A system of guaranteed prices and assured markets was set up under the Agriculture Act of 1947 in order to raise output to a level 50 per cent above its pre-war position, and an attempt is now being made to push production to still higher levels. Although there is now much less reliance on direct price controls, output is still stimulated by government support prices and deficiency payments, the cost of which in 1955-1956 (together with general food subsidies) is estimated at over 335 million pounds. The Ministry of Agriculture through a network of local agencies has extended its work of planning output and guiding farmers in the management of their lands. Although the staff of the Ministry is now greatly reduced from its post-war peak, it remains nearly five times as large as before the war.

Activity to control the location of industry and the use of land is considerably greater than in pre-war days. This effort started on a significant scale as early as 1934 under the Special Areas Acts which offered loans, subsidies, and some preference in government contracts to firms settling in depressed areas. After the war, these powers were revived and strengthened by the Distribution of Industry Acts of 1945 and 1950 and by the Town and Country Planning Act of 1947. These Acts, it was hoped, would lay the basis for public control of land use generally. Under their authority, elaborate machinery for research, planning, and administration has been erected. In consequence of these and supplementary land-use laws and as a result of more vigorous efforts to stimulate housing and slum clearance, the central government has become involved in a wide variety of new activities concerned with land development and building construction.

Compared with the war-time peak of economic regulation, or even with the controls maintained by the Labour Government during the immediate post-war period, present direct controls over prices, production, and distribution represent a wide abandonment of regulatory powers. A variety of controls, however, remain, and in some areas they have been extended. The government, moreover, maintains close informal contacts with industry and labor, and its statistical and informational services are more elaborately organized than they were before the war. As a result, the staffs of the regulatory agencies remain much larger than in pre-war years.

The Changing Character of the British Central Government

Through the many fluctuations in the pace of governmental growth, a number of sustained forces have produced a profound change in the character of the state. This change stands out boldly if we compare the situation in the nineteenth with that in the mid-twentieth century. Table 7 shows the net changes in employment between 1914 and 1950. Before World War I, detailed comparisons are difficult to make, but rough indications can be found.

One of the major changes is the decline in the importance of the armed forces. In 1851 they included 80 per cent of those employed by the central government. Since then they have nearly quadrupled in size, but their relative importance has sunk steadily. They accounted for 70 per cent of central government employment in 1891, 55 in 1914, and 39 in 1950 (Table 2 and Table 4, Part B).

The share of the whole staff devoted to defense, however, has declined much less rapidly, because the number of civilians involved in administering the forces and in producing the weapons of war has increased with great speed. In 1851 the civilian defense staffs numbered approximately 10,000-15,000; in 1891, perhaps 25,000; but in 1950 they employed 391,000 persons of whom 123,000 were in administrative and other non-industrial jobs. The share of the total defense staff in 1851 was therefore roughly

TABLE 7

Central Government Employment, 1914 and 1950

| | THOUSANDS OF PERSONS | | PERCENTAGE CHANGE | RATIOS OF SPECIFIED CATEGORIES | | | |
| | | | | To Total Govt. Employment | | To Total Labor Force | |
	1914	1950		1914	1950	1914	1950
					(per cent)		
Defense	469.3	1,080.8	130	65.3	61.0	2.46	4.69
Armed forces	395.0	690.0	75	54.9	38.9	2.07	2.99
Civilian staffs	74.3	390.8	426	10.3	22.1	0.39	1.69
Post Office	189.7	321.8	70	26.4	18.2	0.99	1.39
Traditional services	29.3	97.6	233	4.1	5.5	0.15	0.42
Revenue	20.0	64.0	220	2.8	3.6	0.10	0.28
Central govt., home and legal depts.	8.3	23.5	183	1.2	1.3	0.04	0.10
Foreign and imperial	1.0	10.1	910	0.1	0.6	0.01	0.04
Modern services	30.7	271.5	784	4.3	15.3	0.16	1.18
Social services	8.1	73.9	812	1.1	4.2	0.04	0.32
Trade, industry, and transport[a]	11.1	113.7	924	1.5	6.4	0.06	0.49
Ministry of Labour	4.4	29.9	580	0.6	1.7	0.02	0.13
Economic regulatory agencies	6.7	83.8	1,151	0.9	4.7	0.04	0.36
Agency services[a]	1.5	26.9	1,693	0.2	1.5	0.01	0.12
Industrial staffs	10.0	57.0	470	1.4	3.2	0.05	0.25
Total	718.9	1,771.7	146	100.0	100.0	3.77	7.68

[a] Non-industrial staff only.

85 per cent of central government employment. In 1950 it was still 61 per cent—very little under what it had been in 1914. While defense therefore remains much the most important activity of the central government, its importance now depends heavily on the volume of civilian support required to sustain the combat elements.

The growth of employment by the Post Office is a function of the rate of progress of the British economy, of the changing importance of transportation and communication in its operation, of the share of that work done by the Post Office, and of course of the productivity of postal workers. In the last half of the nineteenth century, all these factors except possibly the last made for a rapid increase in Post Office employment. The economy was growing rapidly; its growth was fostered and molded by more elaborate facilities for moving goods and messages, among which the Post Office was prominent; the postal service was still young and extending the variety and spatial coverage of its activities. Its staff of workers, some 10,000 in 1851, increased about six times by 1891 and absorbed perhaps one-fifth of all central government workers and about three-quarters of the non-defense staff.

Since that time, however, growth has been slower. By the end of the nineteenth century, most modern postal services were already well developed. Only the telephone and overseas wireless service have been added since. The absorption of the telephone service, together with expansion of the economy, more than doubled the staff between 1891 and 1914. In the next twenty years, however, the staff remained nearly constant, a reflection of relative economic stagnation and improving productivity. Through all these years, from 1891 to 1933, the share of the postal service in central government employment nevertheless remained approximately constant, at first because the Post Office was growing rapidly, and in the 1920's and early 1930's because the government at large, like the Post Office itself, for a time ceased to grow.

The decline in the relative importance of the postal service began in the late 1930's. As economic activity improved, a notable increase in the Post Office staff took place, but it was by no means so rapid as that in defense or in what we are calling the modern services of the government. In 1950 the Post Office used only 18 per cent of all central government employees and less than half of the non-defense staff (Tables 4, Parts A and B).

Apart from the Post Office, the branches of the civil government prominent in the middle of the nineteenth century were the ancient departments concerned with foreign affairs, with internal order and justice, and with the collection of revenues. Altogether these employed less than 17,000 people (outside Ireland), and all but some 2,000 were tax collectors. They accounted for only about 7 per cent of the total central government employment but for about half of the staff not involved in defense.[18]

By 1914 the situation had been transformed. In spite of a considerable increase in the budget, the revenue departments had increased only a third since 1851. Presumably this modest increase was made possible by the simplification of the tax structure carried out in the second half of the nineteenth century, when the tariff was all but abandoned and the excise tax confined to a very few commodities. Because other departments of government increased greatly during this period, the traditional civil departments sank to a minor place. By 1914 they were but 4 per cent of the total and less than 12 per cent of the staff not engaged in defense. Since that time the growing burden of tax collection and the increasing complexity of international affairs have caused the traditional services to grow about as fast as the central government as a whole.

The most dramatic and significant change has, of course, been in the importance of the social services and of the agencies regulating economic affairs. In 1851 the social services were represented chiefly by the Poor Law Board, the General Board of Health, and the British Museum. Together with some still smaller agencies, they employed 313 persons. The only regulatory agencies with staffs of any size were the Board of Trade with 103 officials and the Inclosure Commission with 79. Other agencies dealing with reports and records hired a few hundred persons. Starting with so few workers, the years from 1851 to 1914 must have been the period of most rapid relative growth, for by 1914 the modern services employed nearly 31,000 persons, who constituted 4 per cent of government employees and perhaps 13 per cent of the non-defense staff. The most significant period of expansion,

[18] References to the size of various departments in 1851 are based on the 1851 *Census of Population*, "Tables relating to the principal departments of the Civil Service in Great Britain, from returns furnished by the respective offices, etc.," House of Commons, Accounts and Papers, Vol. LXXXVIII, pp. CCCXLIX-CCCL.

however, occurred after the outbreak of World War I. Since that time they have increased their staff by some 240,000 persons, almost eight times the number they previously employed. They absorb 15 per cent of all government workers and nearly 40 per cent of all workers not engaged in defense. Judged by the size of their staffs, the regulatory and social service agencies bear the same relation to the central government today as did the ancient civil departments a century ago.

CHAPTER 5

LOCAL GOVERNMENTS, 1890-1950

The Main Trend of Local Government Employment

THE expansion of the activities of local governments, like that of the central government, can be interpreted very broadly as a response to conditions created by the industrialization of the nation's economy and by the growth of the towns and cities which accompanied it. Not only did industrialization give rise to the bulk of the problems which local governments have attempted to meet, but also the scientific advance on which industrialization was based placed in the hands of governments the engineering, sanitary, and medical skills required to meet the mounting problems of city life. Industrialization also produced the increase in incomes that enabled communities to afford a large expansion in government activity. And, finally, industrialization was associated with the rise of democracy which made it possible for those most in need of government activity effectively to demand it.

There was, however, this difference between the problems that arose for the local authorities and those that fell to the central government: those that faced the local authorities were more elemental, gross, and unequivocal than those that confronted the national government.[1] Sewage, garbage, mud, epidemics, corpses, fire, and burglary are, so to speak, "conditions, not theories." Moreover, many of these conditions are such as to

[1] The difference between the problems of local and national governments is, perhaps, not precisely expressed here, for the local authorities in Great Britain do not enjoy the degree of independence of national control that we take for granted in this country. In Great Britain the local authorities are the creations of Parliament, their powers are conferred on them by national legislation, they derive a large part of their revenues from Parliamentary grants, and they spend a considerable portion of their funds subject to central supervision and in order to meet nationally defined standards. Parliament and the national government have therefore been intimately involved in the solution of local difficulties.

The difference to which the text refers is more precisely described as the difference between the problems which called for action by the national government through the agency of that government and those which called for action by national *and* local governments principally through the agency of the latter. It should be remembered, moreover, that local initiative had a large part in inducing Parliament to establish the necessary institutions of local government and to broaden their powers. In addition, local governments have wide discretion within the limits of the legislation under which they function, and they possess substantial revenue-raising powers of their own.

persuade even determined individualists that governmental action is necessary. It is hardly possible to buy individual protection against epidemics, public nuisance, or unpaved and uncleaned streets, and it is not cheap to buy it against fire or burglary. The need for a considerable expansion of activity by local authorities, therefore, was widely accepted far earlier than was true in the case of the national government. Indeed, the most significant acts of the central government in the nineteenth century were probably the establishment of new local institutions and the support of local activity. The relatively widespread acceptance of the need for expanded municipal activity rendered local government less sensitive than national government to the fluctuating fortunes of political parties and made for steady growth. Nor did the steadily growing local governments feel the impact of wars as much as the national government.

This complex of conditions helps us understand, at least in a general way, some of the broad characteristics of the trend of local government employment since 1890. The rate of growth was very rapid at the beginning of the period, much more rapid than that of central government employment. Thereafter growth continued at a steadily declining rate and without marked fluctuations. By the end of our period, the rate of growth had become quite low and, indeed, far lower than that of the national civil service (see Table 1). Thus, during the first half of this century, the pace of advance of local government has been slackening while that of the central government has been accelerating. This we may attribute in part to the fact that as early as the first decades of the twentieth century, the facilities for meeting many of the most pressing problems of local government had been successfully created, while the mounting public demands on the central government were only beginning to evoke the instrumentalities for increased action at this level. In part, however, it is due to the fact, of which we shall take more notice later, that the central government, either through normal departmental agencies or through the creation of nationalized corporations, has assumed a number of functions which were previously responsibilities of the local authorities.

If our figures are generally correct, a period of rapid expansion of local government staffs begins as early as the second half of the nineteenth century. This was the time during which far-reaching reforms of local governments and extension of their powers took place.[2] In the years between 1851 and 1891, employment by local authorities at least quadrupled and may have quintupled. By contrast, the civilian personnel of the central government no more than tripled if we treat it in the aggregate; its numerical growth was even smaller if we exclude the Post Office.[3]

The decade 1891-1901, in which our period of special study begins, was one of extremely rapid growth of local employment. According to our estimates, staffs approximately doubled in these ten years (Table 8).[4] Thereafter, there was a steady decline in the percentage rate of growth (see Chart 5). Between 1931 and 1938, the total staff increased only some 10 per cent. And though employment by the local governments rose markedly during the war, by 1950 it had been cut back so far that it stood only 12 per cent higher than in 1938.

The rapid, although declining, rate of expansion of local authority personnel between 1891 and 1931 raised the share of such employment from 1.2 to 5.9 per cent of the labor force (Table 8). But since 1931 the share of the working population absorbed by local government has hardly changed. The great increase in government's absorption of manpower since 1931 has been in the central government.

By the same token, local governments' share in the total personnel used by government at all levels first rose and then declined (Table 1). In 1891, local governments used just one-third of all the men engaged in British government work, including the armed forces. Until 1931, local government grew so much more rapidly than the central government that its share rose to 61 per cent. By 1950, however, it was down to 44 per cent even if we neglect the recent nationalizations. If we take them into account, the local authorities' share in total public employment falls to 25 per cent.

[2] See *A Century of Municipal Progress*, Harold J. Laski, editor, London, G. Allen, 1935.

[3] See table of employment, Chapter 2, note 21.

[4] Information about local government employment, representing as it does the operation of a multitude of agencies, is understandably less satisfactory than that for the central government. For the Census years 1891 and 1901, we have had to estimate major fractions of the total (see the appendix notes to Table 8). Throughout the period covered by Table 8, the functional breakdown is far less detailed than that available for central government employment.

TABLE 8

Local Government Staffs, Selected Years, 1891-1950

	INCLUDING UNEMPLOYED					EXCLUDING UNEMPLOYED				
	1891	1901	1911	1921	1931	1931	1938	1945	1948	1950
	Thousands of Persons									
Utilities	20-30	50-60	138.4	202.8	242.9	226.2	250.0	225.0	270.0a	134.0
Education	30-50	150	214.4	256.6	276.4	273.1	274.7	252.6	281.8	329.8
Police	44.7	50.1	59.4	71.4	70.9	70.4	66.8	71.3	66.8	70.0
Other	55-75	100-140	248.2	444.8	672.6	582.8	681.5	945.1	1,153.4	888.2
Poor relief and institutional staffs[b]	n.a.	n.a.	33.6	50.5	126.6	122.4	n.a.	n.a.	n.a.	n.a.
Miscellaneous	n.a.	n.a.	214.6	394.3	546.0	460.4	n.a.	n.a.	n.a.	n.a.
Total	150-200	350-400	660.4	975.6	1,262.8	1,152.5	1,273.0	1,494.0c	1,772.0c	1,422.0
	Per Cent of Total Local Government Employment									
Utilities	14.3d	14.7d	21.0	20.8	19.2	19.6	19.6	15.1	15.2	9.4
Education	22.9d	40.0d	32.5	26.3	21.9	23.7	21.6	16.9	15.9	23.2
Police	25.5a	13.4a	9.0	7.3	5.6	6.1	5.2	4.8	3.8	4.9
Other	37.1	32.0	37.6	45.6	53.3	50.6	53.5	63.2	65.1	62.5
Poor relief and institutional staffs[b]	n.a.	n.a.	5.1	5.2	10.0	10.6	n.a.	n.a.	n.a.	n.a.
Miscellaneous	n.a.	n.a.	32.5	40.4	43.2	40.0	n.a.	n.a.	n.a.	n.a.
Total	100.0	100.0	100.0	100.0	100.0	100.0	100.0	100.0	100.0	100.0
Total as percentage of working population	1.2	2.3	3.6	5.0	5.9					
Total as percentage of all employed workers						6.2	6.2	6.2	7.9	6.2

a Prior to the nationalization of the electricity supply industry on April 1, 1948.

b 1911: Employment in Poor Law agencies. 1921 and 1931: Employment in all types of municipally owned institutions.

c Excludes civil defense and fire service, which were national functions in these years, as follows: 1945—56,000; 1948—24,000.

d Percentages based on mid-points of range.

CHART 5

Number of Local Government Workers Employed in Various Functions, Selected Years, 1891-1950

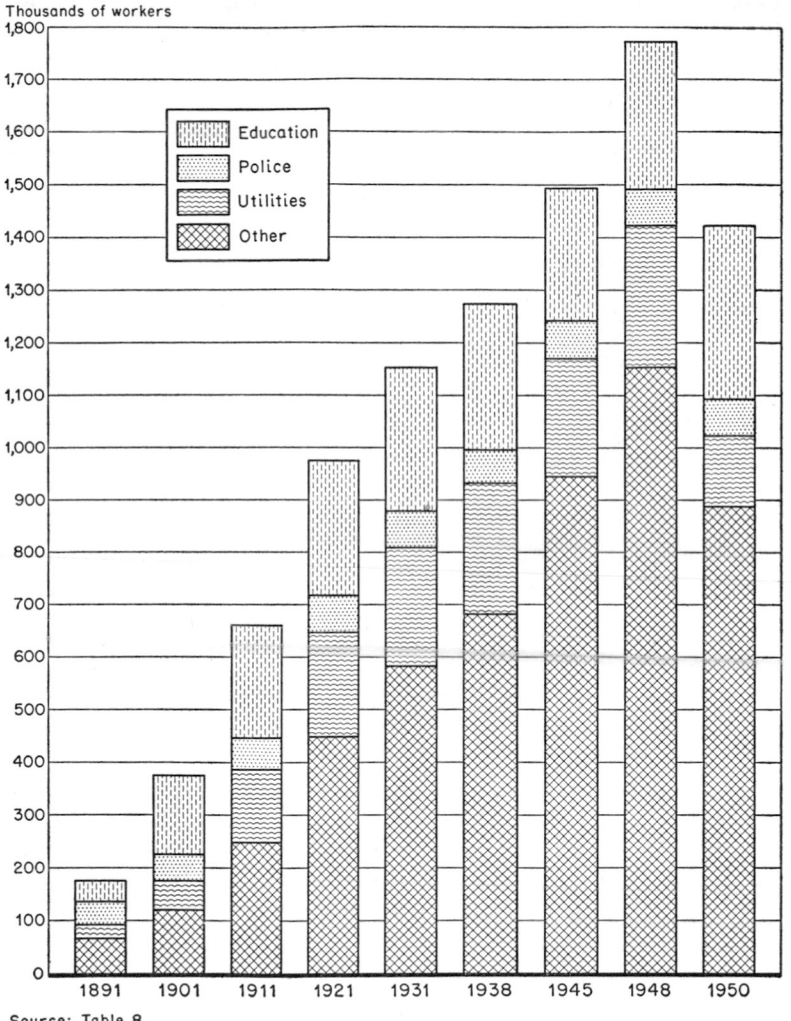

Source: Table 8.

A CLASSIFICATION OF LOCAL GOVERNMENT FUNCTIONS

Some light can be cast on the manner of local government expansion by grouping local activities into four classes:[5] (1) the

[5] We here follow the classification devised by J. H. Warren, "Local Government," in *British Government since 1918*, London, G. Allen, 1950, pp. 196-197.

71

protective services—chiefly police and fire protection; (2) the communal or *environmental services*—tax-paid facilities which benefit all and which do not involve service to selected individuals, for example, sewage disposal, refuse disposal, street cleaning and lighting, parks, and road maintenance; (3) *personal social services*—tax-paid facilities involving service to selected individuals, like education, poor relief, medical care and hospitalization, and housing; and (4) the *trading services* or public utilities—services to individuals or industries provided on a commercial basis. These four groups of services were undertaken by local governments at different times and enjoyed different, although overlapping, periods of rapid development, a fact which helps explain the trend of local authority employment as a whole since 1890. Chart 6 gives the percentage distribution of local government workers according to their functions, insofar as we can distinguish them. The police, however, were the only portion of the protective services which could be isolated, and education was the only separable portion of the personal social services.

1. PROTECTIVE SERVICES

In some, usually rudimentary, form all the services, of course, have existed from time immemorial, but the Police, which dominate the protective services, were the first to be developed in modern form in response to the newer conditions of urban and industrial life. Peel's reform of the Metropolitan Police dates from 1829, and by 1856 the maintenance of an adequate force was made a compulsory local government service, aided by grants from the central government and under the general control of the Home Office. When our study period begins in 1891, there was 1 policeman for every 739 persons in Great Britain. This represented a great expansion of the force since 1851, when there was but 1 policeman for about 1,215 persons. The 1891 standard apparently proved generally adequate to sustain Britain's reputation for orderliness, for by 1950 the ratio had risen only to 1 policeman for every 703 persons. Since the rate of population growth has been declining, the police force, and therefore the protective services generally, have grown at a modest pace since 1890, a pace much slower than that of the remainder of local government.

CHART 6

Percentage Distribution of Local Government Workers among Main Functional Divisions, Selected Years, 1891-1950

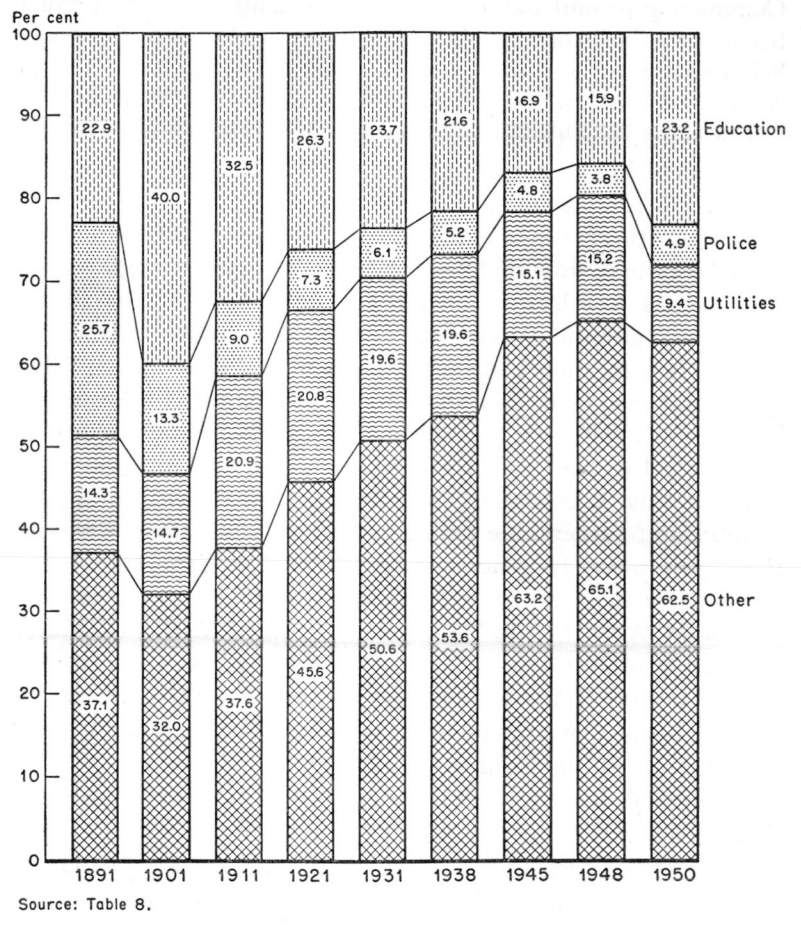

Source: Table 8.

2. ENVIRONMENTAL SERVICES

Two characteristic and important services in this group are the environmental health services and the provision and maintenance of a system of highways and roads. There was rapid expansion in these services in the last decades of the nineteenth and the beginning of the twentieth century.

The environmental health services, in their modern form, got their start in the investigations of the 1830's and 1840's and the establishment in 1848 of a General Board of Health. The legislation of 1848 also provided for the establishment of local health authorities in inadequately supplied localities and for discretionary health powers for borough councils. In 1871 a Royal Sanitary Commission formulated a program of elementary demands which became the basis of a sound sanitary service. It led to the establishment of the Local Government Board and to the Public Health Act of 1875, which created sanitary districts. Since that date the use of public health powers has been compulsory, and progress in this field has consisted mainly in utilizing and extending the powers given by the Act.

In these directions much had already been accomplished by 1890. "By the middle eighties bare essentials for a healthy urban life," writes Clapham, "had already been provided in all the greater communities. Water was abundant and pure. . . . Scavenging, paving, lighting and sewerage were reasonably good."[6] The last cholera epidemic was suffered in 1884. After that, in spite of recurrent threats, neither cholera, nor, indeed, any tropical or sub-tropical disease, became widespread in Britain again.

There was, nevertheless, still much to be done to bring the country up to acceptable standards. For example, the great variation from place to place in mortality rates, especially infant mortality rates, could be explained only by differences in sanitary provisions. As late as 1908 there was evidence that "a very large proportion of the smaller sanitary authorities" were "unworthy of their powers."[7] And even twenty years later the Royal Commission on Local Government heard extremely critical views about the work of the small rural and urban authorities.[8]

Communal health work therefore continued to be pushed, though the rate of expansion declined as the most demanding problems were surmounted. Local expenditures on public health services fell from 8 per cent of total local expenditures in 1913-1914 to 5 per cent in 1947-1948.[9] Since, as we have seen, the rate of expansion of total employment by local governments has been falling, this strongly suggests that there was a significant decline

---

[6] J. H. Clapham, *An Economic History of Modern Britain*, London, Cambridge University Press, 1938, Vol. III, pp. 452-453.

[7] Statement by the Chief Medical Officer of the Local Government Board to the Poor Law Commission. Cited in Clapham, *op. cit.*, p. 436.

[8] William A. Robson, *The Development of Local Government*, London, G. Allen, 1931, p. 302.

[9] These figures exclude expenditures on hospitals, sanatoria, and maternity and child welfare, which we classify as personal services.

in the rate of growth of the staffs occupied with public health work.

The provision of roads had been much neglected during the Railway Age. The coming of motor transportation therefore required a considerable extension and improvement of the highway, road, and street systems of the country. This must have accounted for a very rapid expansion of local employment after 1900, and especially after 1920. Moreover, it seems likely that that expansion would have continued into the present under the pressure of mounting motor traffic if the major highways of the country had not passed under the jurisdiction of the central government in 1934 and if the use of private cars had not been set back by the war. As it is, the advance of local authority highway employment has probably slowed down in recent decades and may even have declined in absolute numbers. Data on manpower are lacking, but the share of expenditures for highways, streets, and lighting fell from 14 per cent of local government expenditures in 1913-1914 to 6 per cent in 1947-1948. Since total employment by local government has been increasing at a steadily slower rate, this again suggests a rapid decline in the rate of growth of the work force in this field.

3. PERSONAL SOCIAL SERVICES

This area of local government activity began to grow substantially only after 1890. At the turn of the century, these activities were still largely undeveloped, but they grew rapidly and account for the greatest part of the expansion of local government employment during the last fifty years. Their growth is connected mainly with four developments: First, the central government in 1902 made itself fully responsible for public education and entrusted the detailed administration of the school system to the local authorities, who, in turn, were instrumental in improving the quality and extent of education. Next, the content of the public health services underwent a profound change, and their emphasis shifted from environmental to personal health services. Third, the old system of public assistance was gradually reformed and replaced by a system of insurance, pensions, and home relief. And, finally, the local authorities took a growing interest in housing and became the main instruments for carrying out the modern housing program.

a. Education. The 1890's had brought in compulsory attendance and free public education at the elementary level in England and Wales. The Act of 1902 put the teachers of the voluntary (i.e. denominational) schools on the payrolls of the local education authorities, which at one stroke more than doubled the public teaching staffs. At the same time, local education authorities were established universally. (The earlier local school boards had been set up only where existing educational facilities were judged inadequate.) Moreover, they were now definitely charged with the development of secondary and technical education.

The result of this combination of events was that the educational staffs of local authorities were five times larger in 1911 than in 1891. Thereafter, however, while expansion continued, it was at a slower rate. It was only some 50 per cent larger in 1950 than in 1911. There were many reasons why the growth of the education staff slowed. On the one side, the ratio of teachers to students rose markedly. In 1901 the local authorities provided only 1 teacher for each 43 students. By 1950 the average was 1 teacher for each 27 students, an improvement of some 60 per cent.[10] There was also a notable approach to universal attendance in the elementary grades. In 1901, only 76 per cent of the children between 5 and 14 were in government-supported schools; in 1950, 92 per cent were in attendance. Secondary school education, however, remained limited. The local authorities provided virtually no secondary school facilities in 1901; but even in 1950 only 10 per cent of all children between 15 and 18 were attending public schools. Thus the proportion of children between 5 and 18 attending schools provided by the local authorities rose only from 55 to 69 per cent, an increase of 25 per cent. Finally, the population development in Great Britain since 1901 has produced an actual decline in the number of children of school age. These were only 86 per cent as numerous in 1950 as in 1901.

As a consequence of these varied influences, the pace of expansion of the educational staff declined. As a fraction of local authority employment, education reached its zenith in 1901, when it comprised 40 per cent of the local government staff.[11] By 1950 education accounted for only 23 per cent of the total.

[10] These and the other figures in this paragraph are drawn from Table 14; see Chapter 7.

[11] This assigns to local authorities the voluntary school teachers who were transferred to their payrolls only in 1902.

b. Personal Health Services and Poor Relief. In the nineteenth
century, government's provision of personal health services was
virtually limited to facilities for paupers. The Poor Law Guardians
provided not only shelter but also infirmaries and medical officers
for their charges. For the non-pauper poor, however, there were,
with some exceptions, only the inadequate facilities provided by
voluntary hospitals. With the gradual elevation of standards and
the growing political power of the working class, the Poor Law
facilities began to be supplemented rapidly by the general provision of health care by local authorities. The school medical
service of 1907 grew into a system of supervision of the health
of all school children, administered by the local education authorities. Many Poor Law infirmaries were transformed over a
period of years into general hospitals, and local authorities became hospital authorities with power to extend public hospital
facilities. Special hospitals for infectious diseases were built,
and general hospital facilities were multiplied. In 1912 a service
for the detection and treatment of tuberculosis was established.
The Lunacy Act of 1913 created a new service for mental de-
fectives. In 1919 the Maternity and Child Welfare Service was
founded.

The relief of destitution proper remained a responsibility of
the Guardians of the Poor until 1929, when their functions passed
to Public Assistance Committees of county and borough councils,
a move designed to enlarge the unit of administration. Under
the pressure of rising standards and of the unemployment of the
1920's and 1930's, the general problem of destitution became
more pressing. On the other hand, there was a tendency for
responsibility to shift from the local to the central authorities.
The establishment and extension of health and unemployment
insurance and of old age pensions marked the advent of this
tendency. It went further during the Great Depression when
the local authorities' responsibilities for the relief of the unemployed who had exhausted their rights to insurance were transferred to the National Assistance Board.

By 1931, local authority institutions and hospitals had come
to have a staff of 126,600 persons. This was four times as large
as that in 1911 and included 10 per cent of local employment.
These figures, moreover, do not include all those involved in
personal health care, but only the institutional staffs.

77

A drastic change in the extent and administration of the social services took place shortly after World War II with the passage of the Family Allowances Act of 1946, the National Insurance and National Health Service Acts of 1946, and the National Assistance Act of 1948, which established an integrated, centrally administered system of social services. For the local authorities of Great Britain, these new or greatly enlarged schemes brought a severe reduction in their responsibilities in this area. Under the National Health Service Act all hospitals and maternity homes which had been established and run by local authorities were taken over by Regional Hospital Boards answerable ultimately to the central government. Many of the functions and institutions which had been developed locally in connection with the school medical service were transferred to the National Health Service. The National Assistance Board took over the home relief and institutional care of persons who formerly were dealt with under the Poor Law. And the entire problem of relief was minimized by the extension of the insurance and pension schemes. The new schemes, it is true, laid certain new responsibilities on local government—domiciliary nursing services and accommodations and care for the aged and blind—but these duties in no way matched those of which the local authorities were relieved. The extent of the shift may be gauged from the fact that the hospitals and other institutions which were removed from local jurisdiction had staffs numbering more than a quarter of a million persons.

Thus the changes in social legislation that achieved the final breakup of the Poor Law and its replacement by a modern system of social services simultaneously established the predominance of central agencies in an area which for centuries had been the domain of local authorities.

c. Slum Clearance and Housing. The activities of local authorities to improve housing facilities began in the 1850's. The early acts, however, merely extended the powers of the local governments to acquire land and unsuitable buildings and to arrange for new housing by selling or leasing the cleared land to private builders willing to undertake to provide substitute housing. Not until 1890 were municipalities enabled to acquire land by compulsion; not till 1909 were they empowered to undertake construction on their own account; and not before 1919 did the national government provide subsidies to support slum clearance and housing schemes.[12] Although the process of clearing slums and providing new working-class housing had gotten well under way before World War I, the work was still on a small scale.[13]

The severe housing shortage after World War I led to a radical change in policy. The government imposed on local authorities definite responsibility for the good housing of workers and granted them subsidies to build new houses. Between 1919 and 1930 some 1.5 million houses were built for rent and about 2.5 million for sale. The former were built mainly by or for local authorities, the latter by private builders.

The supply of housing accommodations suffered during World War II from the cessation of new building, from lack of normal repair, and from heavy bomb damage. After the war, new housing became a first priority of domestic policy. Within the post-war housing schemes the local authorities were made the main instruments for carrying through the government-subsidized building program. The vast majority of the 900,000 permanent and 150,000 temporary houses erected between 1945 and June 1951 were built by them. True, these governments normally operated through contractors, but in June 1951 about 22,000 construction workers were directly employed by them. In addition, the local governments have a multitude of other functions connected with housing. They are owners and managers of huge housing developments, sometimes comprising more than 50,000 houses. They select tenants on the basis of need, fix and collect rents, maintain and repair buildings. They provide and supervise recreation facilities, run restaurants and canteens, provide laundry service, and sell furniture to their tenants. They conduct welfare and educational programs.[14] Finally, the local governments have been assigned extensive responsibilities in connection with town and country planning and the location of new construction of all types.

4. TRADING SERVICES

Local authorities in Great Britain have been heavily involved

[12] Sir Gwilym Gibbon and Reginald W. Bell, *History of the London County Council, 1889-1939*, London, Macmillan, 1939, pp. 364-365.

[13] Of the 87,000 dwellings owned by the London County Council in 1938, only 9,984 had been provided before 1919 (*ibid.*, p. 374).

[14] As early as 1938, the London County Council employed some 2,800 persons as estate managers and maintenance workers, apart from headquarters staff (*ibid.*, p. 394).

in utilities enterprises since the middle of the nineteenth century. Water supply became a common municipal enterprise after the Public Health Act of 1875 made the provision of a proper water supply an obligatory responsibility of the local government. Many cities had acted earlier. By 1911, local government waterworks employed 75 per cent of the labor in the waterworks industry. By 1931 the level of employment had doubled, though the government share remained constant. Since that time there has been little change in the numbers employed.

Local governments became concerned with the gas supply in the last quarter of the nineteenth century. Though the proportion of the industry which came under government ownership was smaller than in the case of water, by 1911 the number of local authority workers in this field was 29,000, and by 1931 it was nearly 38,000. Here, too, employment grew much more slowly after 1931.

At the end of the nineteenth century, electricity came into use, and, after their experience with the gas supply, local authorities entered the new field rapidly. By 1911, municipal electricity systems employed 56 per cent of the labor in the industry. Thereafter municipal employment grew with the rapid growth of the service. Employment rose 450 per cent between 1911 and 1931 and doubled again by the end of World War II.

In local passenger transport, another rapidly growing field, the share of the local authorities was still greater. Over 40,000 were employed on tramways in 1911, and over 73,000 in 1931. Despite the incursion of motorbuses, which remained largely in private hands, the total employment in the municipal tramway and bus service probably stood at about 125,000 in 1948.

In the late 1940's, on the eve of the nationalization acts, between 250,000 and 300,000 local government workers were employed in these four most important utility industries. This represented a five- or sixfold increase since 1900. The share of utilities in the local government labor force had risen to about 20 per cent by 1911. It remained stable till 1938 and declined somewhat thereafter. This development of municipal government, however, was cut short, at least temporarily, by the recent nationalization acts. These resulted in the transfer to national or regional corporations, answerable ultimately to central authority, of all electricity and gas works and of a portion of the local street transport industry. The nationalization of electricity and gas supply alone removed about 125,000 persons from local government payrolls and brought employment on local utilities down to less than 10 per cent of the labor force of local authorities.

The Major Functions and the General Trend
of Local Government Employment

We have suggested above that the growth of local government employment was a response to the major forces operating during the modern period, that is, the interconnected development of industrialism, urbanization, the rise in per capita income and the shifts in political opinion and the locus of political power. This response expressed itself first in the protective services, intended to control the most obtrusive dangers of urban existence—robbery, disorder, and fire. The environmental health services arrived somewhat later, for a variety of reasons: the conditions they were meant to control were less obvious; it was necessary for science to establish the relation between, say, disease and urban waste, or germs and disease; before governments could act, practical means of control had to be found; and, finally, the problems impinged primarily on the poor, while, at least during most of the nineteenth century, Parliament and local bodies were controlled by the rich.

The personal social services—education, medical care, and housing—came still later. Here the benefit to the general public was least obvious though not necessarily least important, and the private interest of the individuals affected was most apparent. The supply of these services therefore at first took on the cast of charity. Means tests were imposed and liberal provision was viewed with suspicion. It took a longer time for the social interest to become evident and for standards of public responsibility to develop. Since personal service is expensive compared with environmental facilities, its provision tended to wait for incomes to rise. Thus the expansion of local government started with services like that of the police, which are of direct benefit to rich and poor alike, and only later moved toward services of direct benefit mainly to the poor, like public education, medical care, and housing.

The trading services, of course, differ from the others. Municipalities took over utilities in response to industrialization of a special kind. Utility services are natural monopolies because

81

they are carried on most efficiently by a single enterprise in a given area. And since they provide services directly to the public, they deal in a market in which the buyers are poorly informed and relatively powerless to protect their own interests. Strict regulation or public ownership has for long been almost universally accepted as the method for handling the problem.

In Great Britain, the alternative of public ownership has often been adopted, for a variety of reasons: a desire to extend facilities more rapidly and widely than private companies were disposed to do; the inadequacy of early regulation of rates and quality of service; the hope of achieving more efficient operation by eliminating rival concerns; a desire to provide the basic necessities of water, light, and transport cheaply to all; and in some quarters a belief that municipal utility ownership afforded a convenient and practicable avenue of advance to socialism generally. As already indicated, the acceptance of these views gradually became wider during the last quarter of the nineteenth century, and the extent of municipal ownership grew on that account and as the utility industries themselves expanded.

If this line of argument is generally correct, it helps us understand the declining rate of growth and the changing composition of local government employment since 1890. For in the case of public services, as in the production of most articles of private commerce, it would seem to be valid to recognize two stages of growth. In the first the service expands swiftly as its major technical potentialities are realized and as its use is accepted by—or applied to—a wider and wider segment of the population. Thereafter, the opportunities for developing a service tend to become narrower. In addition, it sometimes meets the competition of newer ways to perform the same function, as national health and unemployment insurance, for example, have operated to limit the need for poor relief. In its later stages of development, therefore, the growth of a service generally takes place more slowly as its quality is refined, as population and per capita income increase, and as standards rise. At the turn of the century, the protective services and, to a lesser extent, the environmental and trading services had already enjoyed a considerable period of development. Only the personal social services, chiefly education, medical care, and housing, were standing at, or just passing beyond, the threshold of government responsibility. It seems understandable, therefore, that total employment by local government should have grown after 1900 at a declining rate and that the relative importance of the personal service group should have increased.

The Drift toward Centralization

The declining rate of growth of the local government staff in the twentieth century, however, cannot be entirely explained by the fact that a very considerable development of local government had already occurred during the previous century. There has also been a progressive tendency for the central government to assume a larger role in performing functions originally conceived to be responsibilities of local authorities. In one sense this process can be discerned early in the development of modern British government. It is clearly apparent in the nineteenth century in the creation of the Poor Law, police, and sanitary and education inspectorates, and in the expanding system of national grants-in-aid. But these early initiatives of the central government were designed precisely to stimulate and enlarge the activities of the local authorities by expanding their powers and duties, by prescribing minimum standards, and by providing financial assistance. Without this prodding and encouragement from the center, the expansion of local government in the nineteenth century would have been slower.

After 1900, however, the central government began to take actions which, far from stimulating local activity, tended to relieve the local authorities of a portion of their burdens. The change first appeared before World War I and again in the 1920's in the establishment of the national insurance and pension schemes by which a portion of the work of relieving destitution was at once regularized and transferred to central administration. It appeared again in the 1930's with the creation of the National Assistance Board to relieve workers who had exhausted their rights to unemployment benefit. In the same decade the system of national trunk roads was also established. The shift is most impressive, however, at the end of our period in the new and more comprehensive insurance and pension schemes, in the central government's assumption of wider responsibility for residual relief, in the national health scheme, and in the transfer of certain municipal public utilities to nationalized corporations.

One reason for this tendency to centralize the administration of governmental functions is no doubt the increasing burden of these functions in recent decades. As the expense of government increases, there is strong pressure for the central government to assume a larger share of the cost, for it can exploit the richest sources of revenue more conveniently. It can levy heavy income taxes and collect them efficiently without driving taxpayers to other jurisdictions; it does not face the difficulty that business firms spill over local government boundaries; and it can, as local authorities cannot, incur sizable deficits for protracted periods. Since there is a powerful tendency for administrative and financial responsibility to run together, there is also a persistent tendency for the central government to assume a larger share of the newer functions of the state.

Side by side with these financial pressures, one may speculate, are the subtler effects of the growing interconnectedness of people's lives that is an aspect of the advance of industrialization, urban concentration, and improved communications. On the one hand, the realization of interdependence fosters a sense of social responsibility for the fate of individuals, suggests the need for a national definition of the degree of that responsibility, and makes people impatient with the uneven assumption of responsibility which accompanies local administration. On the other hand, the sense of unity fostered by interdependence makes people willing to tolerate the redistributions of tax revenues among regions and income classes that are required when common standards are widely applied. The expansion of local government is, therefore, checked, and that of the central government correspondingly accelerated.

CHAPTER 6

THE NATIONALIZED INDUSTRIES
AND SERVICES

Employment in the Nationalized Industries

BETWEEN 1946 and 1950 the transfer of some of Great Britain's most important industries to public ownership involved a notable expansion of government participation in economic life. Loosely stated, the newly nationalized industries and services identified in Table 9 may be distinguished from the bulk of government services by the nature of their functions and the character of their organization. They differ in function in that they are, for

TABLE 9
Nationalized Industries and Services, Employment in 1950

	Thousands of Persons
Coal mining	735.8
Transportation	888.4
Electricity supply	178.7
Gas supply	140.6
Civil aviation	24.0
British Broadcasting Corporation	11.8
Raw Cotton Commission	0.8
Regional board and teaching hospitals[a]	402.5
Total[b]	2,382.6
Total as percentage of the working population	10.3

[a] Includes 365,850 full-time and 91,714 part-time staff. Of the latter the majority are specialists who hold several positions. Two and one-half part-time workers are counted as one full unit.

[b] Excludes the Bank of England, for which employment data were not available.

the most part, engaged in producing commodities or services of a type which a large section of opinion traditionally believed appropriate for production by private enterprise. They differ in organization in that their assets are owned and their operations managed by public corporations[1] enjoying a high degree of freedom of action from ministerial or Parliamentary control.

[1] An exception is the overseas cable and wireless message facilities, which were merged with the Post Office.

To define these differentiating characteristics of the nationalized industries is not to say that they are without precedent in Great Britain. Both the central and local governments have long furnished services and produced goods which either were concomitantly produced privately or were of a type which could easily be entrusted to private enterprise. Municipalized utilities, ordnance factories, and naval shipyards are obvious examples. More broadly, there are virtually no functions of government, with the possible exceptions of justice, defense, and foreign relations, which were not, when first assumed by the state, widely deemed to fall properly within the sphere of private industry or of philanthropic, religious, or occupational groups. All health, sanitation, and educational activities, for instance, were once considered to be outside the domain of government.

The use of the public corporation as a form of organization had also been well explored before World War II. At the local level there were semi-independent agencies of considerable experience, like the Metropolitan Water Board (1902), the Port of London Authority (1908), and the London Passenger Transport Board (1933). At the national level there was the Central Electricity Board, which had been established in 1926 to promote and control the bulk generation of electricity and to develop a nationwide system of main transmission lines. There was also the British Broadcasting Corporation, created in 1927, whose recognized success made its organization a model for the corporations which later were to control the newly nationalized industries. Just before the war the British Overseas Airways Corporation assumed the ownership of Britain's civil aviation industry from Imperial Airways.

The nationalization acts of the recent Labour Government thus do not represent a wholly new departure for the British state, but rather a huge extension of governmental powers into unsettled and controversial areas under a form of organization not unprecedented, but still unfamiliar. By 1950, total employment in nationalized industries controlled by public corporations was some 2.4 million, or slightly over 10 per cent of the British working population (see Table 9). The industries and services included were coal mining; gas and electricity; inland transport by rail, road, and water; civil aviation; wireless broadcasting; the Bank of England; and the medical institutions which became part of the National Health Service. Early in 1951 all major firms of the iron and steel industry passed into public ownership. This nationalized sector employed close to 250,000 workers who are not included in the above total. At the present writing, Parliament, led by a Conservative Government, has acted to return the iron and steel industry to private hands, but the transfer of ownership has not yet been completed. By the Transport Act of 1953, the Transport Commission also was required to dispose of the bulk of its road haulage undertakings.[2]

The number of persons working in industries nationalized since 1945 does not represent a net addition to public employment. A considerable portion of the assets acquired by the new public corporations were obtained from the local authorities to which they had previously belonged. Measured by output, more than one-third of the gas supply industry and about two-thirds of electricity supply had been owned by local governments for years. The greater part of local street transport, the entire London Passenger Transport Authority, and a large part of electricity generation and long-distance transmission had likewise been in public ownership. The same applies to that major fraction of the hospitals which were owned by local authorities and then brought under the National Health Service.

The significance of nationalization is further qualified by the fact that the privately owned portions of the railroad and utility industries had been subject to close regulation. In coal and steel, moreover, government-approved cartels acted in consultation with government departments and fixed prices and production levels.

The degree of public interest and control already asserted before nationalization, of course, acted to limit the extent to which nationalization could by itself alter the mode of operation of these industries. Furthermore, the newly created public corporations were organized so as to ensure them a very large area of freedom from interference by the state. Unlike the regular government departments, they are not under continuous close supervision by Parliament. A Minister may not be questioned about them except on matters of large public interest. The nationalized industries do not present their estimates to Parliament, their

---

[2] In March 1955 it was reported that almost three-fifths of the steel plants transferred to public ownership by the Labour Government had been restored to private hands (Reuters, March 3, 1955). The return of road transport to private hands was largely completed by mid-1955.

revenues do not pass through the Treasury, their expenditures are not controlled by that department, nor does that department take their profits or meet their losses. Public control is exercised principally by the power of the Ministers to appoint and remove members of boards and to give them general directions on matters affecting the national interest. In addition, public corporations are required to publish detailed annual reports and accounts, which are submitted to Parliament.

Nationalization has also made little difference to the position of the work force, which in its formal aspects remains essentially the same as in private industry. With the single exception of the personnel of the cable and wireless service, who were transferred to the Post Office, the employees of the new public corporations were not assimilated into the government service and did not acquire civil service status. Wages and working conditions are determined by collective bargaining between union and corporation. The right to strike is preserved. Workers in a nationalized industry do not name any members of the boards of directors. Almost all these boards do include trade unionists, but only in their individual capacities. Whether public ownership will, in the long run, make some substantial difference in the position of the work force remains to be seen.

Background of the Recent Nationalization Acts

INDUSTRIES AND BANKING

For this impressive expansion of governmental participation in the production of goods and services there is a broad basis in the development of British social and political thought and additional support from the circumstances of the times and the conditions of the particular industries affected. The acts of nationalization were the work of the Labour Party, which came into power in 1945. Though its doctrinal position was prominent, the Party's electoral success and the nation's acceptance of its program were founded on a sweep of opinion broader than Labour doctrine and on circumstantial influences narrower than doctrinal principle.

Socialist theory characteristically holds that the "means of production" should be owned in common. This point of principle has been formally accepted by the British Labour Party at least since 1918.[3] For industries of national scope, this has usually been

[3] See G. D. H. Cole, *A History of the Labour Party from 1914*, London, Routledge, 1948, pp. 53-54.

taken to mean ownership by the state, and, since the Labour Party and Trades Union Congress of 1935, the Party has viewed the public corporation as the proper agency for the state to use in most cases.[4]

The Socialist position rests on the broadest grounds: that a true political democracy is impossible as long as productive capital is privately owned and wealth unequally distributed, and that the efficient use of capital for the general welfare demands public management "for use and not for profit." Public ownership is viewed also as a device for equalizing wealth and income—an important objective in its own right. It is held to give the working-man an interest in the success of his establishment which will raise his morale and so his productivity. Finally, public ownership is regarded as a way to achieve the rationalization of the structure of industry, which is taken to be impeded by the splintering of units of ownership.

These arguments had won wide acceptance among Labour voters from the beginning of the century, but not all Labour supporters were Socialists and the Labour Party itself had never won a majority of votes in the country or of seats in Parliament before World War II. Considerations of somewhat narrower and more particular application help explain the country's acceptance of the Labour Party and its program of nationalization in 1945.

The economic problem which the public regarded with greatest concern as the war drew to a close was the maintenance of full employment. For this purpose it was held that the level of investment had to be high, and that it had to be susceptible to management in order to keep it stable and to direct its location to areas of surplus manpower. The possibilities of achieving these aims would, it was argued, be enhanced if the area subject to direct public control were enlarged by the nationalization of industries accounting for a significant proportion of total investment. The Labour Party's 1945 program made much of these possibilities, and since there was wide public acceptance of the notion of state intervention to control the level and location of investment, it is plausible that these arguments weighed with many people when they considered the nationalization of particular industries urged by the Labour Party.[5]

[4] Austen Albu, "The Organization of Nationalized Industries and Services," *Problems of Nationalized Industry*, W. A. Robson, editor, London, G. Allen, 1952, pp. 74-76.

[5] The effect of the depression on Labour opinion is well described by

Britain wanted a high level of investment not solely to safe-guard full employment, but also to raise productivity. The country's progress had been slow in the inter-war period. There had been a serious loss of capital abroad during the war, the post-war balance-of-international-payments problem was threatening, and the burden of the social welfare program to be undertaken was heavy. But faith in the country's ability to obtain the benefits of free enterprise was limited. Though skeptical of the fruits of nationalization, *The Economist* wrote: "The vision of a completely untrammelled industry achieving new prodigies of enterprise by the method of free competition is nowadays merely a vision. For one thing, comparatively few British industries are competitive. The practices of controlling prices and production and of protecting profit margins have gone so far that a 'market price' is becoming a rare phenomenon."[6] Some weeks later the same journal added: "In 1939, it was an extreme rarity to find a manufacturing industry where anything approaching genuine competition prevailed, where no control was exercised over prices or the scale of production or the conditions of sale—and such exceptions as existed before the war will be found to have disappeared at its end."[7]

Finally, the idea that deliberate measures of industrial reorganization were necessary was widely accepted, not only by labor groups but also by businessmen. Provided the reorganization could be managed cooperatively, the latter saw in it a means to attain both the safety and profits of limited competition and a more orderly and efficient set of technological arrangements.[8]

H. A. Clegg and T. E. Chester, *The Future of Nationalization*, Oxford, Blackwell, 1953, pp. 11 ff. The Socialism of the 1945 program was notably full-employment-oriented in the opinion of its own supporters. See *New Statesman and Nation*, October 14, 1944, p. 248. The need for state control of investment, although not necessarily by nationalization of industry, was widely accepted even in non-Socialist circles. Beveridge's *Full Employment in a Free Society* had made a striking impression. The most authoritative organ of liberal opinion was convinced: "And even if the question of 'imperfect competition' never arose, purposive direction by the organs of the state would be necessary to secure the two objectives of adequate employment and of a balanced location of industry" (*The Economist*, July 22, 1944, p. 104). The wartime White Paper on *Employment Policy* accepted the task as a matter of governmental responsibility (Ministry of Reconstruction, 1944, Cmd. 6527).

[6] July 22, 1944, p. 104.
[7] September 9, 1944, p. 342.
[8] See Clegg and Chester, *op. cit.*, pp. 15-17.

There had already been attempts of varying significance to achieve better organization, partly by state-tolerated cartels and mergers, partly by active state intervention of various kinds. The public utilities—gas, electricity, and rail transport—had, of course, long been regulated as to prices, character of service, right of entry, and other matters. In addition, considerable portions of the gas, electricity, and local street transport industries were in the hands of local authorities. After World War I the concentration of electricity generation and the construction of a national grid had been accomplished under the aegis of a public body, the Central Electricity Board, established in 1926. Railways were run by the state as a national system in World War I. When returned to private ownership in 1921, they were amalgamated into four companies by authority of an act of Parliament, as an alternative to nationalization. When Lord Ashfield, the most powerful figure in London transport, demanded monopoly powers in order to control and coordinate the activities of independent motorbus operators in the metropolis, the Labour Party, led by Herbert Morrison, argued that the monopoly powers should be granted only to a public board. This was a position which private interests found difficult to attack. The bill to establish the London Passenger Transport Board was passed by a Conservative-controlled Parliament in 1933, and Lord Ashfield himself became Chairman of the Board. Between regulated private monopoly and public ownership there was a short and easy path.[9]

Private cartels and mergers in other fields were, as already stated, common. Their professed aim was rationalization. But while many industries were thus able to restrict output and raise prices, shipbuilding and flour milling were the only industries which by their own efforts were able to achieve even the type of rationalization implied in eliminating the less efficient portions of excess capacity. Both operated through private cartels which financed the retirement of capacity by a levy on the industry.[10] In 1934 the steel industry, with the approval of the government, set up a powerful cartel, the British Iron and Steel Federation, which coordinated the activities of a number of existing quota- and price-fixing associations. In return for promised reorganiza-

[9] *Ibid.*, p. 18.
[10] P. J. D. Wiles, "Pre-War and War-Time Controls," in *The British Economy, 1945-1950*, G. D. N. Worswick and P. H. Ady, editors, Oxford, 1952, p. 140.

tion and capital expansion, the government granted a tariff. The tariff and the restriction of capacity raised profits, but reorganization and development were not impressive.[11]

Private action was often inadequate to bring the divergent interests of different firms under control. After the depression of 1929-1932, the support of state authority was successfully enlisted by a few industries. Steel has been mentioned. The Cotton Industry Reorganization Act (1937) set up a Spindles Board to buy up and scrap excess capacity by levies on the spinners. A 1940 act (Cotton Industry Act) established a Cotton Board "to stimulate research and exports; to collect information; and 'to act as a negotiating body on any matters affecting the industry.' "[12] More important, the coal industry, which had been operated but not reorganized, by the government in World War I, was formed into a statutory cartel in 1930 in the hope that reorganization and development plans might be implemented. This produced district selling schemes which regulated output, but neither the cartel nor the Coal Mines Reorganization Commission were able, with their inadequate powers, to overcome the disinclination of independent, cartel-protected owners to amalgamate pits or to invest capital.[13] The nationalization of coal royalties carried through in 1938 could have only a very gradual effect as existing leases expired.

These measures and the attitudes on which they were based must have predisposed a large sector of non-Socialist opinion to accept acts of nationalization. For if monopoly is openly accepted as necessary for the proper organization, operation, and development of an industry, many persons would accept the need for the most intimate and extensive state regulation. It is then more difficult to oppose public ownership as one means by which that regulation can be made effective.

These considerations applied with exceptional force to the major industries actually proposed for nationalization—coal, transport, gas, electricity, and steel. They are "basic" industries and so appealed to Socialists as the areas in which the principle of common ownership of the means of production should first be applied. They account for a substantial proportion of total invest-

[11] *Ibid.* See also Clegg and Chester, *op.cit.*, p. 38.
[12] Worswick and Ady, *op. cit.*, pp. 140-141.
[13] *Ibid.*, p. 131, and Ben W. Lewis, *British Planning and Nationalization*, Twentieth Century Fund, 1952, pp. 55-56.

ment; hence the task of keeping investment expenditure high and stable might be facilitated by nationalization. The transport, gas, and electricity industries, moreover, are the commonest examples of public utilities. That they are clothed with the public interest had been accepted for decades, and intimate regulation and local public ownership of substantial portions of them already were in effect. Parts of electricity generation and long-distance distribution were already nationalized.

All the industries included in the Labour Government program were monopolies by cartel, by merger, or by franchise. There was, indeed, inter-industry competition between rail and road transport and between gas and electricity. But this rivalry was taken to be only a minor limitation upon market power and, at the same time, an obstacle to the rational expansion of the industries affected. Public regulation therefore was viewed as inevitable, and it had already gone far.

Finally, all the industries were held to require radical improvement in organization, capital equipment, or both. Private or local monopolies, subject to such state authority as had been established before the war, had manifestly proven inadequate. The coal pits still required extensive amalgamation and equipment. The railroads, fast losing traffic to trucks, were failing to improve or even adequately to maintain their equipment for necessary services. Local electricity distribution companies required amalgamation into area schemes to permit standardization of current systems, voltages, and methods of charge; to expand distribution, especially to rural areas; and to obtain more efficient load factors by combining the varying use patterns of different localities. The capital equipment of all the industries on the nationalization list required improvement and enlargement, and government assistance would, it was argued, be required to obtain the capital. In all cases but steel, these needs were defined and certified by a series of public inquiries. In the case of steel the industry produced its own plan for capital expansion with government assistance.[14]

Public opinion with regard to three of the industries was so in accord that The Economist could write before the 1945 elections: ". . . on the further issue of economic policy, the most that a Labour Government could be expected to do would be to change the formal ownership of the mining, transport and power

[14] Cf. Clegg and Chester, op. cit., pp. 20-40.

industries, while a Tory Government will certainly have to concern itself with the same industries, and might well be compelled by events to be almost equally drastic in its intervention in their policies, even though it left the formal façade of ownership untouched."[15]

Nationalization, then, appears to have been only in part a reflection of the spread of Socialist convictions in Britain. In part it must be attributed to the existence of peculiarly difficult problems in a few industries, in part to an attempt to facilitate general employment policy, and in good part to the weakness of private enterprise. The principle, as distinct from the form, of nationalization was accepted with surprisingly little controversy in all the large industries just discussed except steel.

In three other industries there was also little dispute. The Bank of England had been effectively a government organ for many decades. It was brought under state ownership partly to satisfy Socialist principle and partly to clothe it with formal powers to direct the money market. Civil aviation had been nationalized in 1940, when the government took over the monopoly previously granted to Imperial Airways. The industry had been early organized as a monopoly with state subsidy for military reasons, to serve the interests of foreign policy, and because a large scale of operation was thought necessary. It was put under government ownership to permit greater concentration upon national objectives. The Nationalization Act of 1945 merely reorganized the British Overseas Airways Corporation into several area units. Finally, overseas wireless and radio were acquired and placed in the Post Office with the telephone and telegraph services, which the government had taken over many years earlier.[16]

THE HEALTH SERVICE

In addition to passing the acts of nationalization in industrial and commercial fields, the recent Labour Government assumed responsibility for virtually all medical care in Great Britain. This development is again an expression of Socialist principle and the culmination of a long history of expansion in state provision of preventative and curative health services.

In no other field, except perhaps education, does the principle of equal treatment or of provision according to need make such a

[15] May 26, 1945, p. 686.   [16] See above, Chapter 3.

strong appeal. "If the Socialistic principle of the equal treatment of equal needs is to be applied anywhere, medicine is clearly one of the first fields in which it ought to be introduced. In many fields we can fairly salve our consciences, at any rate for the time being, by applying the principle of the 'national minimum' below which no one is to be allowed to fall; we can tolerate large differences above the minimum. . . . But in the case of medicine the minimum is bound to approximate to the standard."[17]

The assumption of some degree of governmental responsibility for public and individual health long preceded the conscious formulation of modern Socialist doctrine and won acceptance far beyond Socialist or Labour circles. In Chapters 4 and 5 we have already traced some of the major steps taken by the central and local governments since the beginning of the nineteenth century, first to provide the proper environmental conditions at home and at work and then to furnish facilities for individual care, particularly through general, tuberculosis, and mental hospitals. In addition, since 1911 the health insurance scheme has provided free medical treatment and sick pay for workers.

Nevertheless, serious deficiencies in facilities for health care were still deemed to exist in the 1930's, and these led to a widespread demand for a comprehensive health service to be instituted after the end of the Second World War. The elaborate survey made by *Political and Economic Planning* in 1937 seemed to bear out three contentions: the standard of health was still low, the incidence of ill health was more general and more serious in the lower income groups, and the existing health services were inadequate. Insurance, for example, covered workers but not their families. A great quantity of disease remained uncared for, even unsuspected. Hospitals were too small, generally below an acceptable standard, and poorly distributed, and other aspects of health care were poorly organized.[18]

The existence of this mass of ill health was, by the early 1940's, regarded not only as an affliction for the individuals involved, but also as a burden on the productivity of the nation and a serious complication for another task which the government was exploring, the creation of a comprehensive social insurance plan.

[17] *New Statesman and Nation*, March 30, 1946, p. 224. See also R. A. Brady, *Crisis in Britain*, University of California Press, 1950, p. 354.

[18] See the summary of the *PEP* and other relevant reports in Brady, *op. cit.*, pp. 355-367.

Sir William Beveridge formulated his scheme for social insurance upon the assumption that there would be a comprehensive national health service providing every citizen "whatever medical treatment he requires, in whatever form he requires it, domiciliary or institutional, general, specialist or consultant, and to ensure also the provision of dental, ophthalmic and surgical appliances, nursing and midwifery and rehabilitation after accidents."[19]

That Beveridge was able to base his insurance scheme upon so radical an assumption is a reflection of the development of public opinion. The British Medical Association had itself proposed a radical extension of health insurance in 1930. The Association put forward a revised scheme in 1938, which, it is estimated, would have entitled at least 90 per cent of the population to free medical care. The Conservative Party, in a Coalition Government White Paper of 1944, accepted, in the words of a spokesman, "the principle of a national, comprehensive, 100 per cent health service."[20] When the Labour Government proposed its plan for a national health service, controversy centered, therefore, not on the general principle, but on such matters as the status of physicians as fee-paid contractors of the service, rather than as civil servants; the degree of professional influence in administration; the role of local governments in the management of hospitals; and the preservation of foundation assets in the case of voluntary hospitals taken over by the state.

The National Health Service Act fell into three main parts. First, the hospitals, both voluntary and local authority, were taken over by the Ministry of Health to be administered by regional hospital boards. Second, for purposes of medical care outside hospitals, the services of doctors, dentists, oculists and opticians, and pharmacists were contracted for on fee bases peculiar to each of these services. These professional services are administered by executive councils, one for each branch of the service. Third, the local authorities were required to provide and maintain a system of health centers to the satisfaction of the Minister of Health. All these services were made completely free to every member of the population choosing to use them,[21] and free choice of physicians was an integral feature of the plan.

[19] W. H. Beveridge, *Social Insurance and the Allied Services*, Macmillan, 1942, p. 158.

[20] Brady, *op. cit.*, pp. 368-369.

[21] Certain charges for eye glasses and dentures were later instituted.

For the purpose of the present discussion, it should be pointed out that only the section relating to hospitals represents a clear act of nationalization. The buildings and equipment of these institutions became the property of the nation, and their full-time staffs became employees of a national service providing hospital care. Doctors and dentists, however, are generally private contractors. They are remunerated by the state for any patients whom they accept under the provisions of the Health Service Act, but they meet their own costs and their income depends primarily on the number of patients they can attract. They reserve whatever portion of their time they please for private practice. The health centers, though subject to central supervision, remain a local government responsibility. These considerations led us to enter in Table 9 only the staff of the regional board hospitals as employees of nationalized industries and services. Since most practitioners, however, have no real alternative to devoting the bulk of their time to the care of clients of the Health Service, and since, with respect to such clients, their fees are fixed and many of their activities are regulated, one may question whether the difference between their position and that of state employees is fundamental.

The National Health Service today cares for almost the entire population, and almost all members of the professional groups involved are participants.[22] While there may be changes in its form from time to time, there can be little doubt that the basic elements of the service will be retained by future British governments.

[22] In 1950 between 90 and 95 per cent of all general practitioners, over 90 per cent of all dentists, and almost all pharmacists were participating. Approximately 95 per cent of the population was using the service (*Health Services in Britain*, British Information Services, T.D. 753, December 1951).

CHAPTER 7

COMPARISON OF GOVERNMENT EMPLOYMENT IN GREAT BRITAIN AND THE UNITED STATES, 1900-1950

THIS chapter makes use of the data furnished by Solomon Fabricant[1] for the United States to make certain comparisons between the levels and trends of government employment in this country and in Britain. The purpose of the comparison is rather narrowly descriptive, because a serious attempt to explain the differences we observe would raise questions too far-reaching for the present study. Nevertheless, by way of affording perspective at various points, we introduce measures related to government employment that we believe are of significance in comparisons of governmental activity in two or more countries, for example, measures of population, labor force, national income and urbanization.

It should also be remembered that, since our figures concern only one type of resource—namely, labor expressed in terms of numbers of employees—they cannot tell us much about differences in the output of government services in the two countries. Equal numbers employed at a given time do not mean equal output, for output depends also on the amount and quality of capital equipment, on efficiency in organization, on the effort and skill of the workers, and on the number of hours they work. Similarly, parallel trends in the numbers employed do not mean parallel trends in output because the trends of changes in labor productivity may have been dissimilar.[2]

As to hours of work, the evidence suggests that, at least so far as the central governments of the two countries are concerned, the work week in Great Britain was about the same as or a little shorter than in this country near the beginning of the century. In the United States it has since then probably become somewhat

[1] Solomon Fabricant, *The Trend of Government Activity in the United States since 1900*, National Bureau of Economic Research, 1952.

[2] Fabricant has described the numerous ways in which the productivity of an hour of government labor time has been raised in the last half-century in the United States by the introduction of a larger volume of capital equipment and by an increase in its efficiency (*op. cit.*, Chap. 5). There has been a similar development in Britain, but measurement of the change in output per man-hour is not practicable in either country.

shorter. In Great Britain, on the other hand, it is now longer than around 1900 and longer than in this country.[3]

[3] For the United States, Fabricant notes that while the average reduction in hours of labor between 1900 and 1940 was between 20 and 30 per cent, it is doubtful that the reduction for government employees was nearly so large. He cites the facts that some government workers—soldiers and sailors, for example—have no fixed hours, that the average public school year was lengthened, that the regular work week of federal employees in the District of Columbia has changed but little from the 39 hours that prevailed in 1900-1903. Although there is evidence of a reduction of hours in most government posts since 1900, Fabricant doubts that the decline can have been as great as the 20 or 30 per cent characteristic of private industry (*op. cit.*, pp. 84-85).

In Great Britain there have been but few changes in nominal working hours of central government employees. In 1890 a 42-hour week was prescribed for the clerical grades generally. This involved a 7-hour day for 6 days a week, but included a lunch interval of unspecified length. Some departments, however, had already begun to grant a Saturday half-holiday in alternate weeks. This was made general by an Order in Council of January 1910. With allowance for lunch and half-holidays, the standard work week was therefore in the neighborhood of 36 hours early in the century. The actual work week, however, was always longer in the provinces and usually longer for most London employees.

During World War I, 51 hours per week were worked, but in 1920 the Civil Service National Whitley Council agreed on a week of 42 hours, including lunch, in London and of 44 in the provinces, to be worked in 5½ days. This standard became effective somewhat later and remained in force until World War II.

Beginning May 1941, hours were increased to 51 per week, and many grades worked these hours through the war without overtime pay. In July 1945 the Treasury asked the Departments to aim at a 48-hour standard week, and in February 1947 it was agreed that the standard week should be reduced from 48 to 45½ hours, to be worked in 5½ days. These hours were still generally in effect at the beginning of 1954 (see *Introductory Memoranda Relating to the Civil Service*, submitted by the Treasury, to the Royal Commission on the Civil Service, Appendix I to Part I of Minutes of Evidence, 1930, pp. 34 and 37-42; *The Whitley Bulletin*, January 1953, and May 1954; and G. Routh, "Civil Service Pay, 1875 to 1950," *Economica*, August 1954).

In addition to the number of hours for which civil servants are in attendance there is a question concerning the pace of work. In Great Britain at any rate there is a suggestion that this has grown more intense. Mr. Guy Routh writes: "There is evidence to suggest that, within the prescribed hours, some departments once afforded ample time for recreation, literary work or simple meditation, but that others, in particular the Post Office, demanded a good deal of application from their servants. In some offices, most of the work seems to have been left to the lowest-paid and least secure members of the staff.

"As in so many walks of British life, the first world war marked the end of a broader and more leisurely era. It is probable that the number of literary and scientific works privately produced at Treasury expense has declined radically and that the modern Civil Servant has to put in a good deal more effort than his Victorian counterpart in exchange for his pay" (*op. cit.*, p. 203).

Our employment figures, moreover, do not furnish an exact comparison of the total quantity of labor absorbed in the production of government service, for they do not measure the number of workers employed indirectly by government as a result of government purchases of goods and services from private industry. Strictly speaking, therefore, our figures indicate only the comparative number of workers directly in the employ of governmental agencies. Presumably these figures give some indications of the total absorption of labor, direct and indirect, by the two governments and of the output of government services. But we cannot tell how reliable these indications are until more comprehensive measurements of government activity in Britain, such as are afforded by data on total expenditure, are available.[4]

Comparability of the Data

Table 10 presents a summary view of the development of government employment in the two countries. The figures in the table reduce the available information to a form which is as comparable for the two countries as we could make it and which affords as much comparable detail as the sources permit. Some differences in the meaning of the figures remain, however. These are negligible for some categories, and we consider them of minor importance for the level and trends of the sum totals. But they are of considerable importance in particular sections of the table, and we try to allow for them where they seem important. The reader, of course, needs to know how the table is constructed in order to form an opinion about the reliability of the comparisons we make. Detailed descriptions of the British figures are provided in the appendix notes to Table 10 and in other tables in this volume from which the data were drawn. The derivation of the American figures is described in detail in the appendixes to Fabricant's volume, as specified in the notes to Table 10.

With some exceptions, we tried to prepare a table which would show for both countries the number of employed persons whose principal occupation was in government or in a government-owned corporation or enterprise. Workers engaged in emergency work relief programs have been excluded, a decision which significantly affects only the 1940 figures for the United States. We have also excluded the employees of nationalized industries

[4] See Chapter 1, note 1, on work by Alan Peacock.

TABLE 10

Total Government Full-Time and Part-Time Employment, and Distribution among Main Types of Government Unit, in Great Britain and the United States, Selected Years, 1900-1950

	U.S. 1900	G.B. 1901	U.S. 1910	G.B. 1911	U.S. 1920	G.B. 1921	U.S. 1930	G.B. 1931	U.S. 1940	G.B. 1938	U.S. 1950	G.B. 1950
	Thousands of Persons											
Federal—U.S.; central—G.B.	312	583	485	614	957	983	820	777	1,532	966	3,526	1,792
National defense	166	458	198	389	581	580	364	419	788	562	2,430	1,085
Armed forces	126	423	140	343	344	475	266	354	532	385	1,673	690
Other defense	40	35	58	46	237	105	98	65	256	177	757	395
Non-defense	146	125	287	225	376	403	456	358	744	404	1,096	707
Post Office[a]	89	85	163	142	195	211	241	223	255	252	354	331
Other	57	40	124	83	181	192	215	135	489	152	742	376
State and local—U.S.; local—G.B.	963	375	1,385	660	1,888	976	2,787	1,153	3,317	1,273	4,054	1,422
School	483	150	596	214	835	257	1,150	273	1,273	275	1,488	330
Non-school	480	225	789	446	1,053	719	1,637	880	2,044	998	2,566	1,092
Total non-defense	1,109	500	1,672	885	2,264	1,379	3,243	1,511	4,061	1,677	5,150	2,129
Total government employment	1,275	958	1,870	1,274	2,845	1,959	3,607	1,930	4,849	2,239	7,580	3,214
	Per Cent of Total Government Employment											
Federal—U.S.; central—G.B.	24.5	60.9	25.9	48.2	33.6	50.2	22.7	40.3	31.6	43.1	46.5	55.8
National defense	13.0	47.8	10.6	30.5	20.4	29.6	10.1	21.7	16.3	25.1	32.1	33.8
Armed forces	9.9	44.2	7.5	26.9	12.1	24.2	7.4	18.3	11.0	17.2	22.1	21.5
Other defense	3.1	3.6	3.1	3.6	8.3	5.4	2.7	3.4	5.3	7.9	10.0	12.3
Non-defense	11.5	13.0	15.3	17.7	13.2	20.6	12.6	18.5	15.3	18.0	14.5	22.0
Post Office[a]	7.0	8.9	8.7	11.1	6.9	10.8	6.7	11.5	5.3	11.3	4.7	10.3
Other	4.5	4.2	6.6	6.5	6.4	9.8	6.0	7.0	10.1	6.8	9.8	11.7
State and local—U.S.; local—G.B.	75.5	39.1	74.1	51.8	66.4	49.8	77.3	59.7	68.4	56.9	53.5	44.2
School	37.9	15.6	31.9	16.8	29.4	13.1	31.9	14.1	26.3	12.3	19.6	10.3
Non-school	37.6	23.5	42.2	35.0	37.0	36.7	45.4	45.6	42.1	44.6	33.9	34.0
Total non-defense	87.0	52.2	89.4	69.5	79.6	70.4	89.9	78.3	83.7	74.9	67.9	66.2
Total government employment	100.0	100.0	100.0	100.0	100.0	100.0	100.0	100.0	100.0	100.0	100.0	100.0

(continued on next page)

TABLE 10 (continued)

	U.S. 1900	G.B. 1901	U.S. 1910	G.B. 1911	U.S. 1920	G.B. 1921	U.S. 1930	G.B. 1931	U.S. 1940	G.B. 1938	U.S. 1950	G.B. 1950
					Per Cent of Total Employment[b]							
Federal—U.S.; central—G.B.	1.1	3.5	1.4	3.3	2.4	5.0	1.8	4.1	3.2	4.7	5.7	7.9
National defense	0.6	2.8	0.6	2.1	1.4	3.0	0.8	2.2	1.6	2.7	3.9	4.8
Armed forces	0.5	2.5	0.4	1.9	0.8	2.4	0.6	1.9	1.1	1.9	2.7	3.0
Other defense	0.1	0.2	0.2	0.2	0.6	0.5	0.2	0.3	0.5	0.9	1.2	1.7
Non-defense	0.5	0.8	0.8	1.2	0.9	2.1	1.0	1.9	1.5	2.0	1.8	3.1
Post Office[a]	0.3	0.5	0.5	0.8	0.5	1.1	0.5	1.2	0.5	1.2	0.6	1.5
Other	0.2	0.2	0.3	0.4	0.4	1.0	0.5	0.7	1.0	0.7	1.2	1.6
State and local—U.S.; local—G.B.	3.6	2.3	3.9	3.6	4.7	5.0	6.2	6.2	6.9	6.2	6.6	6.2
School	1.8	0.9	1.7	1.2	2.1	1.3	2.6	1.5	2.6	1.3	2.4	1.4
Non-school	1.8	1.4	2.2	2.4	2.6	3.7	3.6	4.7	4.3	4.9	4.2	4.8
Total non-defense	4.1	3.0	4.7	4.8	5.6	7.0	7.2	8.1	8.5	8.1	8.4	9.3
Total government employment	4.7	5.8	5.2	6.9	7.1	10.0	8.0	10.3	10.1	10.9	12.3	14.1

a Estimated full-time equivalent numbers, rather than part-time, are given.
b As a percentage of the total labor force, Great Britain, 1901-1921.

in Great Britain in 1950 on the grounds that these represent a peculiar group of huge proportions. To offset this omission we take account of these workers at various points in the discussion below.

The United States and British figures are drawn from different kinds of sources and are not equally reliable. Most of the United States data depend on the payrolls of federal government departments and local authorities. Most of the British data, on the other hand, are of Census origin. Our treatment of unemployed government workers is inconsistent, and the same is true of part-time workers. To be consistent would have driven us to use figures for the one or the other country which we think would have been less apt for the comparisons we wish to make than those included in our table.

Total Government Employment

If we leave the British nationalized industries out of account, aggregate government employment appears to have behaved in the two countries in much the same way over the last half-century (see Chart 7). It is true that the rate of increase, taken by itself, was greater in this country than in Britain. Total government employment in the United States in 1950 was nearly six times as great as in 1900. In Britain in 1950 it was only 3.4 times as large as in 1901. However, since population and labor force also rose more rapidly in this country, it is more meaningful to express government employment as a percentage of total employment. When we do so, the difference between the two countries becomes very small, at least so far as net change in the totals over the fifty years is concerned (see Chart 8). In 1900, total government employment in the United States was 4.7 per cent of total employment. The comparable British figure was 5.8 per cent.[5] By 1950 the American government share in total employment was 12.3 per cent, the British share 14.1 per cent.[6] These figures sug-

[5] The British government figure for 1901 includes a small number of unemployed workers. It is therefore expressed as a percentage of the total labor force.

[6] The British figures include part-time workers as full units. The United States figures do the same except for Post Office part-timers, who are reduced to an estimated full-time equivalent (see appendix notes to Table 10). In the United States the ratio of the full-time equivalent number to the figure in Table 10 was 0.91 in 1900 and 0.94 in 1949 (Fabricant, *op. cit.*, Appendix Tables B-13 and B-14). The comparable ratio for the non-in-

CHART 7

Number of Government Workers in Great Britain and the United States, Selected Years, 1900-1950
(including military personnel; excluding nationalized industries in Great Britain and public emergency workers in the United States)

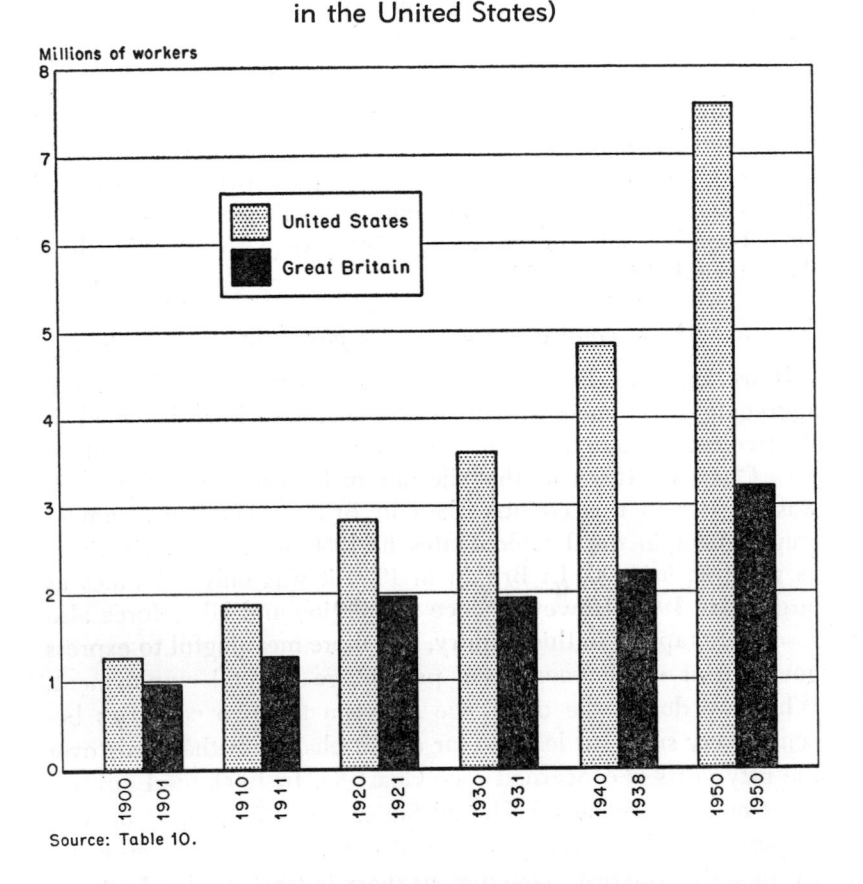

Millions of workers

Source: Table 10.

gest that the share of total employment absorbed by government in Great Britain was a little larger than in the United States but that these shares increased over the half-century in much the same way (see Chart 8). The American share was 81 per cent

dustrial civil service in Great Britain (central government only) in 1950. was 0.97 (*Annual Abstract of Statistics*, No. 88, Central Statistical Office, London, 1952, Table 133). We lack information about part-time work in Great Britain in 1901, but presumably most part-time workers are excluded in Census figures.

CHART 8

Government Workers as a Percentage of All Employed
Workers in Great Britain and the United States,
Selected Years, 1900-1950
(excluding nationalized industries in Great Britain and public
emergency workers in the United States)

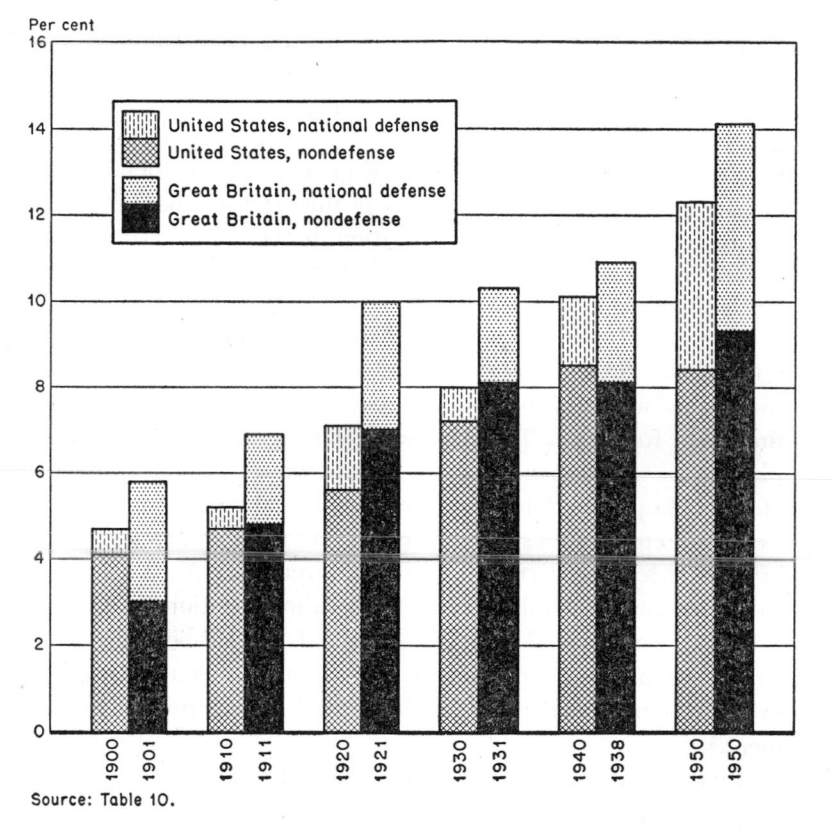

Per cent

	United States, national defense
	United States, nondefense
	Great Britain, national defense
	Great Britain, nondefense

Source: Table 10.

of the British at the beginning of the century and 87 per cent of
the British fifty years later.

This apparent similarity in the level and growth of government
employment in the two countries is subject to certain qualifications. To begin with, the difference between the two countries
is more distinct if we relate the number of government workers
to population rather than to labor force or total employment.
If we think of the ratio of government to total employment as one
measure of resources absorbed, we may think of the ratio of gov-

ernment workers to population as one measure of services provided. Population, labor force, and employment are, of course, closely correlated, but demographic and other influences have combined to keep labor force and employment in the United States lower in comparison with population than has been the case in Great Britain. In 1900, therefore, government employment per head of the population in the United States was only some 65 per cent of the comparable British ratio (see Table 11). On the other hand, employment in the United States grew compared with population at a somewhat faster pace than in Britain. The faster growth of employment relative to population in the United States, of course, kept the share of government in total employment from advancing much faster in this country than in Britain. Expressed per head of the population, however, government employment here rose from 65 to 77 per cent of the comparable British figure.

We must also consider the fact that our figures in Table 10 do not include the nationalized industries in Great Britain. Although this omission is appropriate for many purposes, it may be inappropriate for some. The United States figures include the employees of a number of government-owned trading enterprises engaged in production, trade, or finance, many of them organized as public corporations. Fabricant lists 42 such enterprises owned by the federal government, running from the Alaska Railroad Company to the Rural Electrification Administration. In addition, a host of commercial activities, particularly public utilities, are carried on by local governments. These numerous agencies, however, accounted for only a small fraction of government employment.[7]

If we include all the British nationalized industries, total public

---

[7] *Op. cit.*, p. 106, note. Employment in the public enterprises of the federal government, excluding the Post Office, was approximately 100,000 in 1950; in enterprises owned by state and local governments it was about 250,000. Approximately 50,000 of the latter group worked in industries not nationalized in Great Britain, such as water supply. These workers are, therefore, still included in our British local government figures, while those of electricity and gas works are not. (For employment in U.S. federal enterprises see *Statistical Abstract*, 1951, p. 187, and letters from the Department of Labor to the National Bureau of Economic Research, April 5 and July 21, 1954; in state and local enterprises see *National Income Supplement, 1954, Survey of Current Business*, Dept. of Commerce, Table 26. The total of full- and part-time workers in the state and local category, shown for 1950, is 258,000.)

TABLE 11

Population and the Number of Government Employees per 100 Persons in Great Britain
and in the United States, Selected Years, 1900-1950

DATES		POPULATION (MILLIONS)		GOVERNMENT EMPLOYEES PER 100 PERSONS		GOVERNMENT EMPLOYEES, EXCLUDING NATIONAL DEFENSE, PER 100 PERSONS	
U.S.	G.B.	U.S.	G.B.	U.S.	G.B.	U.S.	G.B.
1900	1901	76.1	37.3	1.68	2.57	1.46	1.34
1910	1911	92.4	41.0	2.02	3.11	1.81	2.16
1920	1921	106.5	43.0	2.67	4.56	2.13	3.21
1930	1931	123.2	44.8	2.93	4.31	2.63	3.37
1940	1938	132.1	46.2	3.67	4.85	3.07	3.63
1950	1950	151.7	49.2	5.00	6.53	3.39	4.33

employment accounted for nearly 25 per cent of total employment in 1950. If we merely add the approximately 418,000 workers in the British nationalized industries who worked for local authority enterprises and institutions before nationalization, the British share of public in total employment becomes 15.9 per cent in 1950. The American share is 77 per cent of that figure. Since it was 81 per cent of the British share at the beginning of the century, it would seem that only if we take account of the bulk of British nationalized enterprises is there evidence that the British government's absorption of labor grew much in the last half-century relative to that of the American government.

The timing of government expansion was also similar in the two countries when measured by percentage changes in the numbers employed by government. In both countries government employment rose at a rapid pace during the first two decades of the century. In the 1920's, after the explosive growth during World War I, the pace of expansion moderated. In the 1930's it was again more rapid in both countries, and it accelerated in the 1940's.

However, the British government absorbed a larger share of additions to the labor force than the United States government over the first half of this century. Between 1900 and 1950, total employment in the United States increased by 34.6 million workers. The rise in government employment was 6.3 million or 18 per cent of the total increase. In Britain, approximately 7.5 million workers were added to total employment, and of these government absorbed 2.25 million or some 30 per cent. In these terms the British government work force grew more rapidly than the American in the first two decades of the century. During the 1920's, and still more during the New Deal 1930's, United States government employment rose more rapidly than British. The British moved ahead again between the beginning of World War II and 1950. During this last period, it may be noted, the American government work force rose 56 per cent, the British 44 per cent. Total employment in the United States, however, increased by 28 per cent, in Great Britain by only 10 per cent.[8] It was the exceptionally rapid growth of total employment in the United States which caused the share absorbed by the govern-

[8] This represents the increase from 1938 to 1950 in Great Britain and from 1940 to 1950 in the United States. On a strictly comparable basis, therefore, the rate of growth was still greater in the United States.

ment of this country to increase more slowly than in Great Britain.

The over-all similarity in the size and rate of expansion of government employment in the two countries also hides important differences in the structure of the government work force and in the rapidity with which its various parts have grown. The distribution of employment between the central government and the local authorities and among the various governmental activities in Great Britain differs from that in this country, and in both respects changes have occurred at a different rate.

Distribution of Employment by Level of Government

At the beginning of the century, government employment in the United States was concentrated at the state and local levels. In Great Britain, on the other hand, the central government employed more persons than the localities (see Table 10). From one decade to another the shares of the central governments fluctuated, but in 1950 total government employment in both Britain and the United States was fairly evenly divided between the center and the localities (including the states in this country).

The differences in the importance of central government in 1900 and the changes over time have been due mainly to the difference between the two countries in the importance of defense employment and to the fluctuations in the volume of such employment between decades. The relative importance of the United States federal government grew between the beginning and middle of the century chiefly because of the great expansion of our armed forces and other defense employment in recent years. In Great Britain the small relative decline in the importance of central government was almost wholly due to the fact that defense employment expanded more slowly than did other types of government employment (compare Charts 9 and 10).

If we eliminate defense employment and calculate the shares of the central government in non-defense employment, the difference between the two countries is far less marked (see Table 12). So restricted, the central government in both countries was a smaller employer than local governments. Moreover, a good part of the remaining difference reflects the greater importance of the Post Office as an employer in Great Britain.[9]

[9] See the section on the Post Office, below.

CHART 9

Percentage Distribution of All Government Workers among Main Types of Governmental Unit in Great Britain, Selected Years, 1901-1950

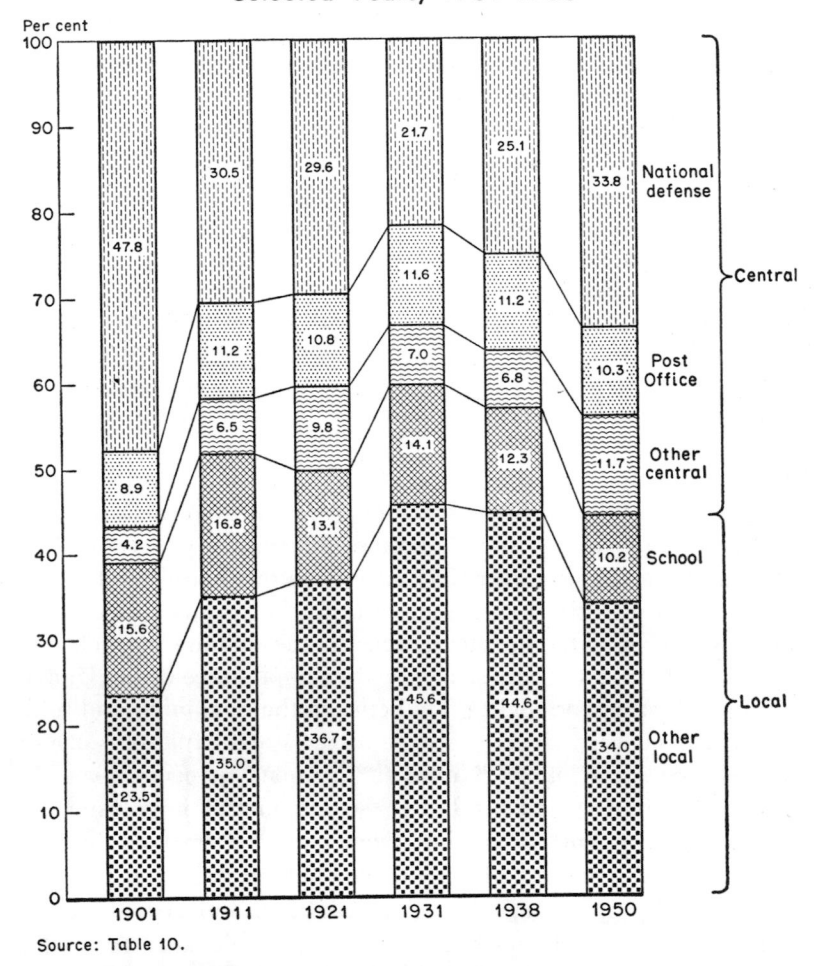

Source: Table 10.

In both countries the substantial rise in the central government's share of total government employment for purposes other than defense occurred in relatively recent times. In the United States the federal share was not much higher in 1930 than in 1900. In Great Britain it was about the same in 1938 as at the beginning of the century. Since those dates, however, the importance of the central government has grown markedly in both

110

CHART 10

Percentage Distribution of All Government Workers among
Main Types of Governmental Unit in the United States,
Selected Years, 1900-1950

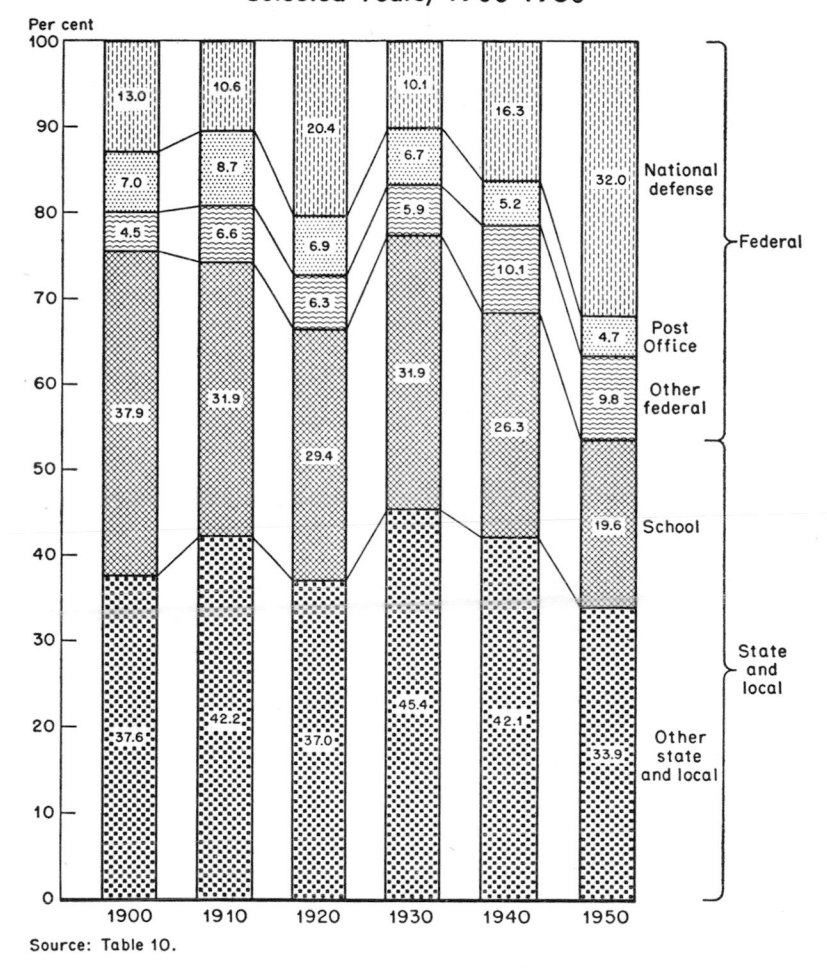

Source: Table 10.

countries. And the reasons were generally similar. The central
government's economic activities as regulator or producer were
greatly expanded, and its participation in social welfare activities
augmented. In part this represented the establishment of new
functions or the enlargement of old central government activities.
In part it represented the assumption by the central government
of functions previously handled by the local authorities. In addi-

111

TABLE 12

Share of Central Government in Total Government Employment in Great Britain and in the United States, Selected Years, 1900-1950

(*per cent*)

DATES		TOTAL CENTRAL IN TOTAL GOVERNMENT EMPLOYMENT		CENTRAL NON-DEFENSE GOVERNMENT IN TOTAL NON-DEFENSE GOVERNMENT EMPLOYMENT		CENTRAL NON-DEFENSE, EXCLUDING POST OFFICE, IN TOTAL NON-DEFENSE GOVERNMENT EMPLOYMENT EXCLUDING POST OFFICE	
U.S.	*G.B.*	*U.S.*	*G.B.*	*U.S.*	*G.B.*	*U.S.*	*G.B.*
1900	1901	24.5	60.9	13.2	25.0	5.6	9.6
1910	1911	25.9	48.2	17.2	25.4	8.2	11.2
1920	1921	33.6	50.2	16.6	29.2	8.7	16.4
1930	1931	22.7	40.3	14.1	23.7	7.2	10.5
1940	1938	31.6	43.1	18.3	24.1	12.8	10.7
1950	1950	46.5	55.8	21.3	33.2	15.5	20.9

tion, the share of the British local governments was reduced in recent years by the transfer of more than 400,000 workers to nationalized industries.[10]

Growth of Employment by Function

While there is much interest in the over-all magnitude of government employment and in its division among the various levels of government, controversy centers chiefly around the state's assumption of unfamiliar duties. To throw some light on the comparative experience of the two countries, we must examine employment by function. This investigation will also illuminate some of the reasons for the great growth of total government employment in the two countries. And since some functions are performed largely by the central governments and others by the local authorities or states, it should also help us understand the distribution of employment among the different levels of government.

Our data enable us to separate the armed forces and other defense workers, the Post Office, and the public schools from the remainder of employment by the central and local governments. The categories we can distinguish are relatively old and well-accepted areas of government activity. The residual employment, both central and local, is a mixed bag. It contains some of the ancient as well as the newer functions. Apart from defense activity the latter account for its great expansion in recent years, so that in an important sense it is around the undefined residual that interest especially revolves. We begin, however, with a discussion of the functions which can be detached from this residual.

NATIONAL DEFENSE

In 1900, United States armed forces were still very small. Although our total government employment was, in absolute numbers, over 30 per cent larger than Britain's at that time, her armed forces were over three times the size of ours. Ours included only 10 per cent of the government work force and only one-half of 1 per cent of all workers employed. Britain's Army and Navy enrolled 44 per cent of government workers and 2.5 per cent of her whole labor force.[11]

---

[10] See Chapters 4-6, above.

[11] In the years compared, both countries maintained forces considerably larger than they had done a few years earlier. The United States had already

Britain, however, was near the summit of her power at the turn of the century, while this country was only beginning to be drawn into a chronic state of international conflict. Our armed forces have, therefore, grown far more rapidly than Britain's. Ours were twelve times larger in 1950 than in 1900, Britain's only 60 per cent larger. The share of our armed forces in government employment rose to 22 per cent, that of Britain's forces fell to the same figure.[12]

We must remember, however, that a large number of civilian employees in both countries are engaged in national defense either as officials and clerks in the service departments or as workers in government-owned munitions establishments, naval shipyards, and the like. The number of these workers rose rapidly in both countries, but, compared with the size of the armed forces, the expansion was far more rapid in Great Britain than in the United States. The relative growth of the civilian element devoted to British defense, therefore, somewhat offsets the slower increase in her armed forces.[13]

The more significant contrast is between all defense personnel, uniformed or civilian, and all non-defense personnel. At the beginning of the century, the total number of defense workers employed by the British government was 2.8 times the number in this country. Such work absorbed 2.8 per cent of the labor force in Britain against only 0.6 per cent in the United States. By 1950, however, government defense workers in the United States had become 2.2 times as numerous as in Britain. They absorbed 3.9 per cent of our total employment against 4.8 per cent in Great Britain.

It emerges, therefore, that although total government employ-

---

emerged from the Spanish-American War, but the military establishment was not cut back to pre-war size. Before the war our forces included some 40,000 men; in 1898 we had 184,000; in 1900, 126,000. The British in 1901 were still engaged with the Boers, and Britain's Army and Navy totaled 423,000 compared with 249,000 in 1891. The difference between British and American forces would therefore have been still greater had our comparisons been pushed back to the early 1890's.

12 After 1950, both countries again expanded their uniformed personnel. Ours more than doubled, standing at nearly 3.5 million at the end of 1953. Britain's had increased to 866,000 by the middle of 1953.

13 In 1900 the figures suggest that there were 3.1 soldiers and sailors for each United States civilian government worker engaged in defense. According to our very shaky guess, the British ratio for 1901 was 12 to 1. Obviously, the precise figures for the early years are not to be depended on. By 1950 the United States ratio had become 2.2 to 1, the British ratio 1.7 to 1.

ment in Great Britain absorbed a larger proportion of the labor force in 1900 than was true in this country, non-defense services absorbed a decidedly smaller share in Britain than in the United States—in the ratio of 3 to 4. By 1950 the position was reversed. In the United States, government employment for non-defense purposes was 8.4 per cent of total employment. In Britain it was 9.3 per cent. Expressed per head of the population, the number of government workers in the United States fell from 109 to 78 per cent of the comparable British ratio (see Table 11). Moreover, the British share would be larger if we added the workers transferred from local authorities to nationalized industries.

This change indicates a considerable net expansion of government non-defense employment in Britain relative to the United States. But if we exclude the nationalized industries there is little in the figures to show that the difference may not be temporary. The British share increased relative to the American from 1900 to 1920. The United States share increased relative to the British from 1920 to the end of the 1930's, and just before World War II it exceeded the British share. The final relative rise in Britain was achieved only during the 1940's. During this last period, moreover, the governmental non-defense staffs of both countries increased at the same rate—27 per cent.[14] But the exceptionally large rise in total United States employment kept the ratio of the government non-defense work force stable in this country while the British ratio rose.

THE POST OFFICE

In both the United States and Great Britain, the post office has been a substantial employer. In this country it has accounted for something between 5 and 7 per cent of total government employment in this century, while in Britain the post office share has been between 9 and 11 per cent. In both countries it accounted for more than half of the non-defense staff of the central government until relatively recently.

There have, however, been significant differences between the two countries as regards the size and growth of their post office staffs. By comparison with its total labor force, the British staff has been substantially larger than the American. An important part of the explanation is that the British Post Office includes the

[14] This again covers the period from the last pre-World War II years: 1938-1950 in Britain, 1940-1950 in the United States.

country's telephone and telegraph service while the American does not.[15] To measure the effect of this difference in scope, one could, in principle, either raise the American or lower the British figures by the number of telephone and telegraph workers in the given country. In fact, only the first adjustment is possible, for a large number of British Post Office personnel attend both to postal and telegraph business, and the Post Office reports do not allocate their services. Table 13 compares the share of the British Post Office in total employment with that of the United States Post Office, unadjusted and after adjustments to include telephone and telegraph workers. The adjusted figures for the United States give us, in effect, a post office of British scope.

These figures permit us to say unambiguously that the United States communications industry made a larger direct drain on manpower than did the British. United States employment in communications was much larger in absolute numbers and somewhat larger relative to total employment. But we cannot say with assurance that, relative to total employment, the staff of the United States postal service proper was larger or smaller than that of the British postal service proper. We can say that telephone and telegraph employment in the United States increased more rapidly than did postal employment proper (see Table 13). It seems very likely that this was also true in Great Britain. If so, it helps account for the fact that the share of the British Post Office in total employment rose faster than did the share of the United States Post Office. We must remember, however, that the difference in the scope of functions of the post offices of the two countries is not the only difference between them. There are also differences in their load of work due in part to the radically different economic geography of the countries and to the size and composition of their output. And there are differences in service, mechanization, organization, and labor efficiency which we are in no position to measure.

EDUCATION

Employment in public educational institutions accounts for a large identifiable block of workers under the jurisdiction of local government in both countries. Table 10 suggests that such work

[15] The British Post Office did not finally absorb the private National Telephone Company until 1912, but before that it was responsible both for telegraph service and for long-distance telephone service.

TABLE 13

British and American Post Office Staffs, and American Telephone and Telegraph Workers, Selected Years, 1900-1950

		THOUSANDS OF WORKERS				PER CENT OF TOTAL EMPLOYMENT[b]		
		United States			Great Britain	United States		Great Britain
		Post Office	Telephone & Telegraph Industries	Post Office & Tel. & Tel. Industries Combined		Post Office	Post Office & Tel. & Tel. Industries Combined	
U.S.	G.B.							
1900a	1901	89	106	195	85	0.3	0.7	0.5
1910a	1911	163	221	384	142	0.5	1.1	0.8
1920a	1921	195	359	554	211	0.5	1.4	1.1
1930	1931	241	432	673	223	0.5	1.5	1.2
1940	1938	255	364	619	252	0.5	1.3	1.2
1950	1950	354	605	959	331	0.6	1.6	1.5

a Figures for United States telephone and telegraph industries represent employment in 1902, 1912, and 1922.
b As a percentage of the working population in Great Britain, 1901-1921.

has consistently absorbed a larger share of total employment in the United States than in Great Britain. The American share was almost twice the British in 1900; it was still two-thirds greater in 1950. These results are, in some respects, in accord with our expectations, since it is well known that public education was far better developed by 1900 in the United States than it was in Britain. However, public education has been greatly expanded in Britain in this century, and might have been expected to require a comparable share of the labor force.

Government's demand for teaching manpower depends, of course, on a wider range of considerations than the phrase "the development of public education" suggests. The portion of total employment absorbed by public education is determined by the following relations:

- The ratio of the school-age population to the total number of employed persons
- The ratio of the number attending school to the school-age population
- The ratio of public to private school attendance
- The ratio of teachers and others employed in public education to the number of students

It must not be supposed that these measures are completely independent of one another. There is, for example, much flexibility in the number of students who can be taught by a single teacher. An increase in the number attending school may be offset by a decline in the teacher-student ratio. Nevertheless, our understanding can be improved by a consideration of the ratios just described or measures closely approaching them. The relevant figures are summarized in Table 14.

In 1900, persons occupied with public education in the United States comprised 1.8 per cent of all persons employed. In Great Britain, grant-aided schools absorbed slightly less than 1 per cent of total employment.[16] In part this difference was due to the fact that in the United States a larger proportion of children between the ages of 5 and 18 were actually attending government-supported schools. The British ratio was only 82 per cent of the American. The difference was largely on the level of the elementary school, but not entirely so. Public secondary educa-

[16] This refers to the situation after the passing of the Education Act of 1902 which put teachers of voluntary schools on the payrolls of the local education authorities.

TABLE 14

Measures Bearing on the Use of Manpower for Education,
Great Britain and United States, 1900 and 1950

	U.S. 1900	G.B. 1901	U.S. 1950	G.B. 1950
1. Total public employment in education (thousands)	483	150	1,488	330
2. Teachers in full-time public schools (thousands)				
Elementary and secondary	423	138[a]	914	238
Colleges and universities	n.a.	n.a.	106	8[b]
Total			1,020	246[b]
3. Total employment (thousands)	26,984	15,400[c]	61,630	22,787
4. Ratio of total employment in public education to total employment (per cent)	1.79	0.97	2.41	1.45
5. Ratio of teachers in public elementary and secondary schools to total employment (per cent)	1.57	0.90	1.48	1.04
6. Ratio of teachers in full-time public schools to total public employment in education (per cent)				
Elementary and secondary	87.6	92.0	61.4	72.1
Total	n.a.	n.a.	68.5	74.5
7. Population of school age (thousands)				
Ages 5-14	16,954	7,791	24,410	6,713
15-18	6,118	2,962	8,486	2,562
5-18	23,072	10,753	32,896	9,275
19-22	5,883	2,873	8,911	2,711
8. Enrolled students, all regular schools (thousands)				
Ages 5-14	16,262	n.a.	22,202	6,313
15-18[g]	699	n.a.	6,427	311
5-18	16,961	n.a.	28,629	6,624
College and university	238	n.a.	2,659	103
9. Enrolled students, all regular public or grant-aided schools (thousands)				
Ages 5-14	14,984	5,907	19,404	6,157
15-18[g]	519	18[d]	5,707	266
5-18	15,503	5,925	25,111	6,423
College and university	n.a.	n.a.	1,355	n.a.
10. Ratio of school-age population to total employment (per cent)				
Ages 5-14	62.8	50.6	39.6	29.5
15-18[g]	22.7	19.2	13.8	11.2
5-18	85.5	69.8	53.4	40.7
19-22	21.8	18.7	14.5	11.9

(continued on next page)

119

TABLE 14 (continued)

	U.S. 1900	G.B. 1901	U.S. 1950	G.B. 1950
11. Ratio of students in government-supported schools to all students (per cent)				
Ages 5-14	92.1	n.a.	87.4	97.5
15-18g	74.2	n.a.	88.8	85.5
5-18	91.4	n.a.	87.7	97.0
College and university	n.a.	n.a.	51.0	n.a.
12. Ratio of students in government-supported schools to school-age population (per cent)				
Ages 5-14	88.4	75.8	79.5	91.7
15-18g	8.5	n.a.	67.3	10.4
5-18	67.2	55.1	76.3	69.3
19-22	n.a.	n.a.	15.2	n.a.
13. Ratio of teachers to students in government-supported schools				
Elementary and secondary schools	2.7	2.3e	3.6	3.7
College and university	n.a.	n.a.	7.8	7.7f
14. Ratio of total employment to total population (per cent)	35.5	41.3	40.6	46.3
15. Ratio of total employment to population 19 years and over (per cent)	61.5	69.1	60.1	63.7
16. Ratio of population 5 to 18 years to total population (per cent)	30.3	28.8	21.7	18.8

a Includes 1,136 secondary school teachers in Scotland.

b Includes teachers in private as well as public universities.

c A crude estimate used in order to avoid comparing employment in teaching with the total labor force unadjusted for unemployment. For lack of a better basis, we assumed the ratio of unemployed to labor force was the same in Great Britain as in the United States. We think the error is probably smaller than that involved in using the unadjusted labor force figure.

d Scotland only.

e Cmd. 8244 (1951), Table 95, based on somewhat different data, gives figures equivalent to 2.1 per cent in 1901.

f Ratio of full-time teaching staff to students in all universities.

g The ages for attending high school in the United States are normally 14 through 17. But to avoid complicating the table, we have followed the British practice of splitting the school-age population into the two groups 5 to 14 and 15 to 18.

tion, virtually non-existent in Britain around 1900, was starting in the United States. Over 8 per cent of those between 15 and 18 were attending. Public higher education was also beginning in the United States. Some 4 per cent of those aged 19 to 22 were enrolled in colleges and universities, many of these attending state institutions. Furthermore, the teacher-student ratio was lower in Britain. For the elementary and secondary schools it seems to have been only about 85 per cent of the United States figure.

However, these two factors—the ratio of students in government-supported schools to school-age population and the teacher-student ratio—together account for only two-thirds of the difference between the American and the British share of employment devoted to public education. So far as the data assembled in Table 14 can take us, the remainder of the difference is due to the lesser importance in Britain of the school-age population compared with total employment. In 1900 the ratio of the number of children aged 5 to 18 to all persons employed was only about 82 per cent as large as in the United States. These three factors together appear to account for virtually the entire difference in the relative importance of employment in public education in the two countries.[17]

The smaller ratio of children to total employment in Britain cannot be attributed to a smaller proportion of children of school age in the total population compared with the United States, for, at the beginning of the century, the school-age populations were almost equally important in both countries. The difference must instead be attributed to the fact that in the United States the ratio of total employment to total population was only 80 per cent as high as in Britain. Hence the school-age population was relatively small in Britain compared with total employment and its absorption of manpower for education correspondingly small.

This aspect of the matter is, of course, itself connected with

[17] Let S_a = the ratio of students in government-supported elementary and secondary schools in America to population 5 to 18
S_b = the same in Britain
T_a = the teacher-student ratio in America
T_b = the same in Britain
C_a = the ratio of children 5 to 18 to total employment in America
C_b = the same in Britain

Then $\dfrac{S_b}{S_a}$ (= 0.82) $\times$ $\dfrac{T_b}{T_a}$ (= 0.85) $\times$ $\dfrac{C_b}{C_a}$ (= 0.82) = 0.57

According to the figures in Table 14, the British share of total employment devoted to public education was 54 per cent of the American share.

121

the relatively low proportion of children attending school in Great Britain in 1900. A child kept in school not only requires the services of teachers and others, but after a certain age is himself a loss to the labor force. The forces which made school attendance in Britain less frequent both reduced the demand for teachers and helped increase the number of persons at work. On both counts, therefore, they helped make the portion of total employment devoted to education lower in Britain than it was in this country. There were, of course, other factors that made the British labor force ratio in 1900 larger than the American, but an investigation of them would be beyond the reach of this study.[18]

Fifty years later, the share of total employment devoted to public education was larger in both countries. It had increased one-third in the United States and over one-half in Britain. The British share was 60 per cent of the American in 1950. This increase occurred in spite of the fact that the size of the school-age population declined markedly compared with total employment in both countries. The decline was somewhat greater in Britain and its causes were a little different in the two countries. Though school-age population declined compared with total population in both, the decline was somewhat greater in Britain. Total employment rose in both countries compared with population, but the rise was somewhat greater in the United States. One reason was that school attendance by children over 14 increased in both countries, but the rate of increase was greater in Britain, to the disadvantage of the work force.

In both countries the increased absorption of manpower by public education was due mainly to three factors: a rise in the rate of attendance at government-supported schools, a rise in the teacher-student ratio, and a rise in the ratio of non-teaching personnel to teachers.

With regard to the first matter, the experience in the two countries was somewhat different. The United States in 1900 was already putting virtually all children through a full course of elementary education.[19] The rate of attendance at public ele-

[18] It should be noted, moreover, that the bases of the estimates in 1900-1901 assembled in Table 14 are especially insecure. See also the appendix notes to Tables 10 and 14 for comments on the accuracy and comparability of the data.

[19] In Table 14 the ratio for 1900 is only 88.4 for two reasons: first, ele-

mentary schools actually fell between 1900 and 1950 because of the relative expansion of private, mostly Roman Catholic, schools. On the other hand, there was a great growth of attendance in public high schools and in colleges and universities. In 1950, high school attendance was equal to 76 per cent of the boys and girls between 15 and 18, and nearly nine out of ten were in government-supported schools. In addition, three out of ten persons 19 to 22 years old were enrolled in colleges and universities, and state institutions provided for half of them.

In Britain both the elementary and the secondary schools gained. Elementary schooling was encouraged by a gradual rise in the school-leaving age; by government assumption of the maintenance expenditures of the voluntary schools; by the abolition of fees, which later was extended also to secondary schools; and by an expansion of facilities. Secondary school education was first made a responsibility of local authorities in 1902, so that the period of substantial secondary school growth has been confined to this century. But the expansion of secondary schooling and the increase in attendance at institutions of higher education have been much less than in the United States.

Both countries have raised their ratios of teachers to students over the century, and the British, who appear to have been considerably behind in 1900, may now employ even more teachers per 100 students than do this country's public elementary and secondary schools. A substantial portion of the increase of the work force attached to public educational institutions, however, appear to be due to the rapid expansion of the non-teaching staffs. For this category reliable and complete data appear to be virtually non-existent for the period around 1900, and even for the recent years we have to rely on rough estimates. According to our rather shaky figures the ratio of teachers to other personnel in public schools was approximately 90 per cent at the beginning of the century. By 1950 the non-teaching staffs appear to have increased to about 30 per cent of the total work force devoted to public education. In the United States their share was possibly even greater.[20]

---

mentary education normally ends at 13, but in order to maintain comparability with British data we compare elementary school students with the population aged 5 to 14; second, a fraction of elementary school students attended private schools.

[20] See appendix notes to Table 14.

We also must remember the important development of public facilities for part-time education of young people and adults. But the lack of data does not permit us to trace the demand for manpower of this sector over a long period.[21] It should be noted, however, that the expansion of teachers in these part-time schools, and that of non-teaching staffs generally, appears to account for the entire expansion of the ratio of public employment in education to total employment in the United States. In Great Britain the greater part of the expansion in the ratio is traceable to the same sources. Indeed, it appears that the group which comes first to one's mind if one speaks of the growth of public education—teachers in full-time elementary and secondary public schools—accounted for a smaller share of total employment in 1950 in the United States than it did at the beginning of the century, and for only a slightly larger share in Great Britain (Table 14, Item 5).

It need hardly be stressed that this review of numbers is but an introduction to a large subject. The measurements themselves are incomplete and insecure, especially for the early period. Moreover, the analysis of differences in the use of manpower for public education in the two countries permitted by our figures hardly takes us as far as we might wish to go. It cannot tell us, for example, why secondary schools reach a larger proportion of the teen-age population in the United States than in Britain, why the private elementary school has become so important in this country, or why there is such a great difference in facilities for higher education. We must, however, leave the matter at this point.

The Other Functions of Central and Local Government

After setting apart the portions of employment devoted to defense, to the post office, and to the schools, we come closest

---

[21] In the United States in 1949-1950, 2.6 million persons were enrolled in adult education classes taught by 46,677 teachers. It is not specified whether the latter are part- or full-time (*Biennial Survey of Education, 1948-50*, Federal Security Agency, Chapter 2, Table 12). In the academic year 1949-1950, in England and Wales alone, there were 2.2 million persons registered in further education classes, and there were 17,078 full-time teachers in institutions for further education and special schools and 2,503 teachers in maintained and voluntary training colleges (*Education 1900-1950*, Report of the Ministry of Education for the year 1950, Cmd. 8244, 1951, Tables 33a and 51).

to those elements of government which rouse the sharpest concern at the present time. When people dispute about the scope of governmental activity and the most desirable boundary between the private and governmental spheres, they argue about functions included in this residual category. We are, unfortunately, unable to measure as closely as we should like the size of the area about which argument centers. We must be satisfied with comparing a miscellaneous group which combines some of the most ancient functions of government with its controversial incursions into economic regulation, social welfare, and the production of goods and services. This is awkward, but we may be confident that for Great Britain and the United States, the controversial functions are chiefly responsible for the expansion of the residual category in the last fifty years.[22]

Our estimates suggest a development in the two countries since 1900 similar in its general aspects although different in degree and timing. The figures to which we have particular reference are set out for greater convenience in Table 15. Certain similarities between the two countries are striking. In 1900 almost all employment in this category was at the local (and state) level. In both countries the central governments—apart from defense and the Post Office—were extremely small. United States government employment, by virtue of a relatively large number of workers in the states and localities, exceeded that of the British government as a percentage of total employment. Whether the difference is really significant, however, in view of the shaky character of the estimates for this early year, is at least questionable. Between 1900 and 1950, government employment in both countries grew much more rapidly than did employment as a whole. It appears, indeed, that government employment in both countries grew more rapidly than did employment in any other major sector of the economy. The division of employment between central and local government suggests also a certain similarity in the functions undertaken. In the United States the major growth in the share of government was at the state and local level, until the Great Depression and the problems raised by World War II and its aftermath set in motion a significant relative increase in federal employment. Apart from the decade of World War I, the same trend is apparent in Great Britain.

[22] See Chapters 4-6, above, for Great Britain, and Fabricant, *op. cit.*, Chap. 4, for the United States.

TABLE 15

Government Employment excluding Defense, Post Office, and Education as a Percentage of Total Employment in Great Britain and the United States, Selected Years, 1900-1950

| DATES | | FEDERAL (U.S.) OR CENTRAL (G.B.) EXCLUDING DEFENSE AND POST OFFICE | | STATE AND LOCAL (U.S.) OR LOCAL (G.B.) EXCLUDING EDUCATION | | FEDERAL, STATE, AND LOCAL (U.S.) OR CENTRAL AND LOCAL (G.B.) EXCLUDING DEFENSE, POST OFFICE, AND EDUCATION | |
U.S.	G.B.	U.S.	G.B.	U.S.	G.B.	U.S.	G.B.
1900	1901[a]	0.2	0.2	1.8	1.4	2.0	1.6
1910	1911[a]	0.3	0.4	2.2	2.4	2.5	2.8
1920	1921[a]	0.4	1.0	2.6	3.7	3.0	4.7
1930	1931	0.5	0.7	3.6	4.7	4.1	5.4
1940	1938	1.0	0.7	4.3	4.9	5.3	5.6
1950	1950	1.2	1.6	4.2	4.8	5.4	6.4

[a] Number of workers attached to the British government expressed as a percentage of the working population in these columns.

Along with these general similarities there were also differences. The net increase between 1901 and 1950 in the share of employed labor absorbed by the residual category in Great Britain was somewhat greater than that in this country. While percentage increases calculated upon the small and faulty values for 1900 are bound to be in error, the figures indicate that the central government's share in Britain became more than eight times as large as it had been in 1900; in this country it became but six times as large. The local government share became nearly three and one-half times as large in Britain as it had been fifty years earlier; it became less than two and one-half times as large in this country.

The timing of change in terms of shares of total employment was also different in the two countries (Table 15, last two columns). The British government grew relatively more than the American in the first twenty years of this century, reflecting, among other things, the influence of the Liberal Governments before World War I and the effects of the war itself. The United States government grew relatively fast in the next twenty years—in the 1920's when state and local governments enjoyed the abounding revenues of great prosperity, in the 1930's when the Great Depression and the New Deal combined to produce a great expansion of the federal government. Meanwhile, the growth of the British government was constrained by a policy of strict economy.[23] By the end of the 1930's the modern functions of the United States central government accounted for a larger share of total employment than the British, and the United States share was not much smaller than the British when we combine central and local jurisdictions. It was therefore only the growth connected with World War II and the recent Labour era that gave British government the small margin it held in the early 1950's. A few years hence, the size of the controversial residual category of the central government relative to total employment may very well again be the same in the two countries, as at the beginning of the century.

Table 15 is of special interest, for it is presumably in this residual category, whose size and growth are heavily influenced by the newer activities of government, that the influences connected with industrialization and urbanization, with the level

[23] See Chapter 4, above.

of incomes, and with the evolution of political opinion, are most important. In earlier chapters we have suggested tentatively that a number of concomitants of the process of economic development in Great Britain during the last century or more were largely responsible for the expansion of the modern functions of government. The assembly of large numbers of people in cities, the growth of large-scale industry and its dependence on distant and unstable markets, the altered position of labor, the emergence of new types of monopoly, natural and otherwise, created problems difficult for private enterprise and the unregulated market to handle. The increase of incomes and the enlargement of the natural and social sciences, which were causes and consequences of economic development, provided government with the means for assuming new responsibilities. The growth in the political power of the working classes and of the collectivist policies they adopted to express their economic interests impelled the British government, after a time, to enlarge the scope of its activity. And problems were aggravated and the process hurried on by the effects of the great wars of this century, wars whose impact upon society was unprecedentedly great because of the level of economic development which Britain and other countries had attained.

The application of this thesis is hardly confined to Great Britain. Fabricant, for example, presents a very similar hypothesis for the United States.[24] Though it is not a wholly new thesis, it is not well tested or developed in detail. To test the validity of this argument and its range of application, would require study of many countries over an extended period. Moreover, comparison of Great Britain with the United States shows that the thesis is, at the least, incomplete.

In a general way the facts are consistent with the hypothesis. There has been economic growth in both Britain and the United States, and in both government employment has expanded markedly compared with total employment or with population. Moreover, at least since 1900, when statistical comparison becomes possible, government was the most rapidly expanding major division in either economy, as judged by employment. The presence of a similar powerful cause or set of causes is, therefore,

[24] *Op. cit.*, Chap. 7.

128

clearly suggested, and this is perhaps the chief conclusion to be drawn from the comparisons. But consideration of some objective indications of economic development shows that that process alone does not readily account for all the observed facts. Even as between two countries generally so similar in their political and economic institutions, differences in the size or trend of government employment appear which are not easily reconciled with their relative states of economic development.

International comparisons of income are notoriously inaccurate and misleading. Rough estimates indicate, however, that income per capita in Great Britain and this country were approximately equal in 1900.[25] At the same time, urbanization and industrializa-

[25] United Kingdom:

National income at factor cost	£ 1,803 million[a]
Population	41.15 million[b]
National income per capita	£ 43.81
National income per capita in dollars (£ 1 = $4.866)	$213

United States:

Net national product	$16.02 billion[c]
Population	76.1 million[d]
Net national product per capita	$210

[a] James B. Jefferys and Dorothy Walters, "National Income and Expenditure of the United Kingdom, 1870-1952," mimeographed, a paper submitted to the International Association for Research in Income and Wealth, Third Conference, Castel Gandolfo, September 1953, Table VII.

[b] Registrar General.

[c] F. C. Mills, *Productivity and Economic Progress*, National Bureau of Economic Research, Occasional Paper 38, 1952, Appendix Note 1. The data are based on Simon Kuznets' estimates, revised to include full defense output in national product.

[d] United States Census from *Historical Statistics of the United States, 1789-1945*, Bureau of the Census, 1949, Series B-31.

The figure for Britain is low for purposes of comparison with the United States: (1) Income at factor cost is less than net national product by the amount of indirect business taxes. (2) Per capita income for the United Kingdom is lower than that for Great Britain because it includes Ireland, where incomes were lower than in England, Scotland, and Wales taken together. Allowance for this difference between the estimates for the United States and Britain would reinforce the argument of the text since that requires that per capita income in Britain in 1900 should have been no lower than that in the United States.

The use of the official exchange rate in order to convert British incomes to dollars is a dubious procedure. But it has greater justification for a time of relatively free trade like 1900 than it would today, and greater justification for Great Britain, which is so heavily engaged in foreign trade, than for most countries.

129

tion had proceeded much farther in Britain than in this country.[26] On these grounds we should expect that government activity had attained a higher level in Britain in 1900 than in this country. But judged by the share of the labor force devoted to non-defense activities, the United States government was larger than the British (Table 10). The relative difference is somewhat smaller if we exclude the post office and education, but there is no evidence to support the view that the British share was the larger (see Table 15).

Since 1900, moreover, the pace of economic development has been more rapid in the United States. Average income in this country is now far higher than in Great Britain. While the degrees of urbanization and industrialization remain lower here, the gap has been closing.[27] If there were a simple connection

[26] Some relevant figures follow:

	U.S. 1900	G.B. 1901
Urban population in per cent of total population	40%	76%
Persons per square mile	26	425
Gainfully employed in non-agricultural industry, in per cent of total gainfully employed (U.S.) or working population (G.B.)	62%	91%

Sources: *U.S.*: Census of 1900.

          G.B.: Censuses of England and Wales, and of Scotland, 1901.

[27] As regards incomes, a recent study based upon an elaborate comparison of prices in the United States and United Kingdom gives the following ratios for product per capita in the United Kingdom in 1950 (U.S. = 100):

	U.S. Price Weights	U.K. Price Weights
Gross national product	63	49
Consumption	66	52
Investment	35	31
Government	107	77
Non-defense, total	131	93
Non-defense, personnel	163	163

(Milton Gilbert and Irving B. Kravis, *An International Comparison of National Products and the Purchasing Power of Currencies*, Paris, OEEC, p. 113.) The figures for government are not wholly comparable with those cited in our study since those above exclude government enterprises including Post Office, education, and health services.

As regards urbanization and industrialization in 1950, there are the following figures for comparison with those in footnote 26, above:

	U.S. 1950	U.K. 1951
Urban population as per cent of total population	59	80[a]
Persons per square mile	51	560
Non-agricultural employment as per cent of total employment[b]	87	95[c]

Sources: See footnote 24, above, except as noted below:

between economic development and the size of government and if it had dominated the outcome, the non-defense activities of the United States government would have grown more rapidly than those of the British government between 1900 and 1950. The reverse, however, was true, judging by the share of the labor force absorbed in government work (Tables 10 and 15).

Our comparisons of the growth of government employment in two countries are, of course, only an imperfect and partial test of the connection between economic development and the size of government. A connection might stand out far more clearly in comparisons involving many countries than it does when we compare the experience of any two. Even in a comparison between Britain and United States, we may form a different impression when we can study more comprehensive measures of government's use of resources based on the total expenditures rather than on labor directly employed. Our judgments of long-term trends are, moreover, complicated by fluctuations in the rate of expansion in the two countries. As recently as the end of the thirties, the share of employment absorbed by non-defense activities was greater in the United States than in Great Britain, and that absorbed by the residual category was not much smaller. Ten years from now the United States shares in both categories may be the greater.

Taking the figures at face value, moreover, they do not necessarily imply that the connection between economic development and size of government is weak. They do suggest that the connection is not simple and that other significant forces are also at work. It is plausible to suppose, for example, that growth of government follows economic development only after a more or less protracted interval. Fabricant thought it likely that such a lag has been present in the United States.[28] Similarly, we have suggested in Chapter 2 that the expansion of the British government was retarded in the nineteenth century by the slow pace at which public opinion with regard to government evolved and political power shifted. If there is merit in this notion, the more rapid pace of British governmental growth in the twentieth cen-

a Mid-year estimate of the Registrar General, *Annual Abstract of Statistics*, No. 89, p. 13.
b Employed workers only.
c *Distribution of Total Manpower*, Ministry of Labour, New Series.
28 *Op. cit.*, p. 150.

tury is in part a response to the rapid industrialization in the nineteenth.

We must also consider that aggregate indexes of economic development, such as are afforded by figures on national income, population density, and over-all measures of urbanization and industrialization, are inadequate indicators of the gravity of the problems raised by economic growth in countries whose economic structures are different. Industrial composition and dependence on foreign trade, for example, may influence a country's sensitivity to business fluctuations. The distribution of the population among communities of different size may affect the seriousness of the problems of living within cities as well as those of inter-urban communication and movement. The course of population growth determines the age structure of the population and the size of families and therefore influences the demand for education, medical care, and the support of the aged, as well as the size of the work force itself. The industrialization of foreign economies creates problems whose character and severity depend on a variety of special factors.

Another large consideration is the influence of the great wars of this century. They have economic roots, and their scope and effects are certainly heavily influenced by the level of economic development. But the impact of wars on different countries cannot be measured in reference to general indexes of economic activity. They have borne upon Great Britain and this country with very unequal weight.

Still another complication arises from differences in political arrangements—for example, from the difference between the federal constitution of this country and the more centralized political structure of Great Britain, or from differences in the size and functions of local government units. If certain powers are reserved to the states, as in this country, the economic rivalries of their citizens will influence the pace at which taxes and regulatory activities are enlarged. If there are significant economies of scale in governmental, as in industrial, operations, the size of political units will affect the productivity of labor and the cost of governmental services.

It is, of course, only too evident that the material gathered in this study is not sufficient to enable one to sort out and establish conclusively the importance of the factors that control the general trend of government activity, much less those that account for international differences. For that, the experience of a large number of countries and more detailed information about each will be needed. The international comparisons we have made and the explanatory hypotheses we have entertained were and, indeed, could be no more than incidental and tentative explorations in a study whose aims were more modest—to compile measures of the direct use of labor by the British government and to describe its expansion in the context of a summary of major developments influencing British governmental activity.

APPENDIX

SOURCES AND NOTES TO TABLES

Main Sources

THE main source of information on the total government work force and the total working population in the period 1891 to 1931 is the decennial Census of Population for Britain and Wales and Scotland. These Censuses were taken on April 5, 1891; March 31, 1901; April 2, 1911; June 19, 1921; and April 26, 1931. All Census data cited below refer to these dates.

The five Censuses are not completely comparable because methods of taking and reporting the Census have changed. Before 1891 the Census questionnaires asked only for a person's occupation. In 1891 a question as to status—employer or employee—was added. The 1911 Census contained for the first time a question as to "the nature of the employer's business." This furnished the basis for a more accurate industrial classification, and made possible the identification of industrial workers employed in government-owned establishments. For example, while in earlier Census reports a carpenter working in a government-owned shipbuilding plant was listed only under his occupational group, the 1911 Census reported for the first time—in addition to the non-industrial civil service—the number of industrial government workers.

The 1891 and 1901 Censuses also listed large groups of persons employed by local authorities—school teachers, workers in municipally owned utilities, sanitation, road maintenance, etc.—under only their respective occupational groups and not under the heading "Local Government." Only the 1911, 1921, and 1931 Censuses included a complete count of central and local government workers. For the earlier years the Census figures had to be raised to take account of the omitted categories. The adjustments made in computing our tables are described below.

The Census data on government workers include the unemployed, except in 1931, when a special count of the unemployed was made. They also include as full units part-time workers whose main occupation was in government service.

Since the 1941 Census was omitted because of the war and the 1951 Census does not distinguish between private and public employment, we have to rely on other sources of information on

134

government workers for the period after 1931. These sources are also important in providing detail not furnished by the Census for years both before and after 1931. Data on the armed forces are available from the reports of the service departments. Data on civilian central government employees by department are published at frequent intervals by the Treasury Department. In 1914 the Treasury began to publish the number of all persons —established as well as unestablished—in the non-industrial civil service. From the 1930's on the Treasury returns also list the numbers of industrial workers employed by the central government. These payroll data have certain advantages over Census data: they exclude the unemployed and—though only for the non-industrial civil service—distinguish between full-time and part-time employment.

Comprehensive payroll data, however, are available only for the central government, not for local authorities. For the period after 1931, information on local government employment is incomplete. For certain categories—such as police, or teachers in schools run by local authorities—data are available from the Home Office or the Ministry of Education for England and Wales and the Home Department or the Education Department for Scotland. For other types of local government employment we must rely on estimates. The procedures followed in deriving these estimates are described below.

TABLE 1

ARMED FORCES

Census years—armed forces at home: Data are from Census of England and Wales and Census of Scotland. 1891 and 1901: *Occupation Tables*. 1911: *Occupation and Industry Tables*. 1921 and 1931: *Industry Tables*.

Figures as given in source were adjusted as follows: The 1921 and 1931 *Industry Tables* include under the headings Army, Navy, and Air Force the civilian employees of the War Office, the Admiralty, and the Air Ministry. The staffs of these service departments—reported in the Treasury returns "Staffs Employed in Government Departments," Cmd. 1290, 1921, and Cmd. 3898, 1931—were shifted from Armed Forces to Civil Central Government.

Census years—armed forces abroad: Figures refer to persons born in England, Wales, and Scotland. Data are from War Office, Admiralty, and Air Ministry returns, reported in the Census of England and Wales. 1891: *General Report with Summary Tables and Appendices*. 1901, 1921, and 1931: *General Report with Appendices*.

The Census of England and Wales for 1911, *Volume 10, Part I*, gives the numbers of the armed forces of the United Kingdom at home and abroad, but no information as to the birthplaces of the forces serving overseas. The number of English, Welsh, and Scottish members of the armed forces abroad was estimated at 70 per cent of the difference between the number of the armed forces in Great Britain and the total number of the United Kingdom forces at home and abroad.

1938 and 1950—armed forces at home and abroad: Data are from Ministry of Labour and National Service, "Distribution of Total Manpower, Great Britain," cited in Central Statistical Office, *Annual Abstract of Statistics*, No. 89, H.M.S.O., London, 1952. Figures refer to June of each year.

CIVIL CENTRAL GOVERNMENT

Census years: See sources for armed forces at home.

Adjustments: Figures given in the *Occupation Tables* of the 1891 and 1901 Censuses were raised by 15,000-25,000 for 1891 and 20,000-40,000 for 1901 to take account of industrial government workers not included in the Census data.

1921 and 1931: Civilian employees of the service departments were added to Civil Central Government (see above note on adjustment of data on armed forces).

1938 and 1950: Data are from Treasury returns "Staffs Employed in Government Departments" (quarterly), cited in *Annual Abstract of Statistics*, No. 85, 1948, and No. 89, 1952. Figures refer to April 1 of each year.

Adjustments: One-half of the number of part-time workers in the non-industrial civil service—reported in the Treasury returns—was added to the Treasury totals to obtain the number of full-time and part-time workers. Information about the number of part-time industrial government workers was not available.

LOCAL GOVERNMENT

Census years: See sources for armed forces at home.

Adjustments: Figures given in the *Occupation Tables* of the 1891 and 1901 Censuses were raised by 80,000-130,000 for 1891 and 250,000-300,000 for 1901 to take account of persons in education, municipally owned public utilities, sanitary services, road maintenance, and miscellaneous labor not included in the Census data (see notes to Table 8).

1938: See notes to Table 8.

1950: Estimate by T. M. Ridley in "Note on the Extent of the Public Sector of the Economy in Recent Years," *Journal of the Royal Statistical Society*, Vol. CXIV, Part II, 1950. Based on returns rendered to the Ministry of Labour and National Service by local authorities.

TOTAL WORKING POPULATION AND ALL EMPLOYED

Figures in upper panel include the unemployed and persons temporarily separated from their work. Both panels include part-time workers—each being counted as a full unit—armed forces at home and abroad, and merchant seamen and fishermen at sea.

Census years: See sources for armed forces at home.

Adjustments: Census figures were raised by (a) armed forces abroad (see above) and (b) merchant seamen and fishermen employed on registered British vessels at the date of the Census, but not included because they were at sea. Sources for (b): Data furnished by the Registrar General of Shipping and Seamen, cited in Census of England and Wales. 1891 and 1901: *General Report with Appendices*; 1911: *Volume 10, Part I*; 1921 and 1931: *General Tables with Appendices*.

1938: Data are from Ministry of Labour and National Service, "Distribution of Total Manpower, Great Britain," old series. This series—which reports a total working population of 19,473,000 persons for June 1938—excludes gainfully occupied men over 65 years, women over 60 years, and private indoor domestic servants. The number of persons in these categories was estimated by reference to a study by H. Frankel, "The Industrial Distribution of the Population of Great Britain in July 1939," *Journal of the Royal Statistical Society*, Vol. CVIII, 1945, Parts III-IV, at 3,131,000, and this number was added to the total reported by the Ministry of Labour. To find total employed workers we assumed that the unemployment ratio for the categories added to the old manpower series was the same as for the working population included in this series.

1950: Data are from Ministry of Labour and National Service, "Distribution of Total Manpower, Great Britain," new series. Private indoor domestic servants and gainfully occupied persons over pensionable age who were excluded from the previous series of manpower statistics are included in the new series. Figures refer to June.

TABLE 2

1891-1931: Data are from Census of England and Wales and Census of Scotland. 1891 and 1901: *Occupation Tables*; 1911: *Occupation and Industry Tables*; 1921 and 1931: *Industry Tables*.

Adjustments: Armed forces abroad were added to Census figures for 1891-1931 (see notes to Table 1, above). The estimated numbers of industrial government workers were added to Census figures for 1891 and 1901 (see notes to Table 1).

1951: The final results of the 1951 Census—taken on April 8—were not yet published. The *One Per Cent Sample Tables, Part I* include in the Industry Tables under "Defense" the armed forces at home, the civilian non-industrial employees of the service departments, the military nursing services, and hospitals and similar institutions operated by the armed forces. But these tables do not include a breakdown for armed forces and civilian employees or any information on the armed forces abroad. For these reasons we substituted the figure for the armed forces from "Distribution of Total Manpower, Great Britain," new series, cited in *Annual Abstract of Statistics*, No. 90, 1953.

The Sample Tables report 361,000 persons in civil central government service. This number excludes the non-industrial staff of the service departments (but includes the staff of the Ministry of Supply), the entire Post Office, and all government industrial workers who are reported under their respective Industry Groups. We added the number of Post Office workers from the Census Industry Group "Transportation and Communication." We further added the civilian employees of the service departments (reported in the Treasury return on non-industrial staff in the civil service on April 1, 1951) and the industrial staff in the civil service (as reported by the Treasury Department for April 1, 1951) with the exception of industrial Post Office workers, who are included in the Census data for the Post Office.

Adjustment: The Census figure for total working population was raised by 250,000 to account for armed forces abroad and merchant seamen and fishermen at sea.

137

APPENDIX

TABLE 3

1902: Data are from "Return Showing the Total Numbers of Persons in the Established Civil Service of the State," Treasury Chambers, Cmd. 409, 1902.

1911: *Idem*, Cmd. 210, 1911.

1914: *Idem*, Cmd. 390, 1914.

Adjustments: The staffs of specifically named Irish departments were eliminated. But certain departments, notably the Post Office and Revenue Departments, include Irish employees who could not be excluded.

TABLE 4, *Part A*

ARMED FORCES AT HOME AND ABROAD

Army, 1914 and 1918: Data are from the War Office, *Statistics of the Military Effort of the British Empire during the Great War, 1914-1920,* H.M.S.O., 1922, pp. 29-30.

Includes the Regular British Army, excluding reserves and territorial forces on August 1, 1914; including expeditionary forces, but excluding colonial and native forces in November 1918.

Navy, 1914 and 1918: Data are from H. Newbolt, *History of the Great War Based on Official Documents,* London, 1931, Vol. V, p. 433. Includes H.M. Navy and Royal Marines, excluding reserves on August 15, 1914; including reserves on November 15, 1918.

Air Force, 1914: Royal Flying Corps and Royal Navy Air Force—strength 2,073—are included in Army and Navy. 1918 data are from H. A. Jones, *The War in the Air,* Official History of the War, 1937, Appendix XXXV.

Army, 1928: *The General Annual Report of the British Army for the Year Ending 30th September 1928,* H.M.S.O., Table 1.

Army, 1933: *Idem,* for the year ending 30th September 1933.

Army, 1936: *Idem,* for the year ending 30th September 1936.

The figures for 1928, 1933, and 1936 represent the regimental strength of British troops on the British and Indian establishments, plus headquarters and other staffs of the Regular Army, plus permanent staffs of the Territorial Army and of other reserve formations, less Colonial Corps and Indian Troops borrowed. Figures refer to October 1 of each year.

Navy, 1928, 1933, and 1936: Data are from *Statistical Abstract for the United Kingdom,* No. 82, H.M.S.O., Table 141. Reserve formations are excluded from the totals. Figures refer to March 31 of each year.

Air Force, 1928, 1933, and 1936: *Statistical Abstract for the United Kingdom,* No. 82, H.M.S.O., Table 145. Reserve formations are excluded from the totals. Figures refer to March 31 of each year.

Army, Navy, and Air Force, 1939: Great Britain, Central Statistical Office, *Statistical Digest of the War,* H.M.S.O., 1951, Table 9. Figures refer to June.

Army, Navy, and Air Force, 1945 and 1950: Data are from "Distribution of Total Manpower, Great Britain," cited in *Annual Abstract of Statistics,* No. 88, 1952. Figures refer to June of each year.

NON-INDUSTRIAL STAFFS

1914 and 1918: Data are from "Statement Showing the Staffs of Government Departments on August 1, 1914, November 11, 1918, and March 31, 1919," Treasury Chambers, Cmd. 276, 1919.

The Admiralty figures do not include foreign yards. The Air Ministry figures do not include Depots, etc. The War Office figures do not include Regimental Record Offices, Pay Offices, etc.

Personnel in specifically Irish departments were excluded. Irish personnel in other departments were included; except Post Office, from the staff of which subtractions were made as follows: 1914—staff numbering 21,089 who were in Ireland on March 31, 1914, as given in "Report of the Postmaster General on the Post Office," 1913-1914, Cmd. 7573, 1914. 1918—staff numbering 19,083, which represents the average of the 1914 staff in Ireland and of the staff transferred to the Irish Free State in 1922. The latter figure is given in "Statement Showing the Staff Employed in Government Departments," April 1, 1922, Treasury, Cmd. 1658, 1922.

Figures represent the total of full- and part-time workers; except for the non-industrial staff of the Post Office, for which the sources state the proportion of part-time employees. These were counted one-half.

1928 and 1933: Data are from "Staffs Employed in Government Departments," Treasury, Cmd. 3106, 1928, and Cmd. 4351, 1933.

Adjustments. Staffs of certain outlying branches of the War Office and staffs of Unit and Command Offices, etc., of the Air Ministry were added to the totals for War Office and Air Ministry.

Staffs in all departments were adjusted for part-time workers on the basis of the numbers of part-time workers given in"Statement Relating to the Employment of Ex-Service Men in Government Offices," Treasury, Cmd. 3114, 1928, and Cmd. 4352, 1933.

Total non-industrial staffs were raised to include the staffs engaged on reserved or agency services in Northern Ireland, which numbered 5,004 persons in 1928 and 4,983 in 1933.

1936, 1939, 1945, and 1950: Data are from the Treasury returns "Staffs Employed in Government Departments," on April 1 of each year, cited in *Annual Abstract of Statistics*, No. 84, 1948, and No. 89, 1952.

Staffs of reserved and agency services in Northern Ireland are distributed among the various departments in 1939, 1945, and 1950, but in 1936 appear only in total non-industrial staffs.

Post Office non-industrial staff, 1939, 1945, and 1950, excludes sub-postmasters and sub-postmistresses who numbered approximately 8,000 in each year.

INDUSTRIAL STAFFS

1914 and 1918: Data are from Ministry of Reconstruction, *Fifth Interim Report of the Civil War Workers Committee*, Cmd. 9192, 1918. Shows the estimated number of persons employed in government-owned establishments in July 1914 and January 1918. The figures include workers in Ireland, but exclude government workers in Forestry and industrial workers in the Post Office.

The industrial staff as shown in the above source was divided between Defense and Miscellaneous Industrial Staffs by reference to Census figures for England and Wales in 1911. These showed some 35,000 industrial industrial government workers employed in establishments of a military character and some 6,000 others. It was assumed that defense workers would have increased more rapidly than non-defense workers between 1911 and 1914 and that the latter remained constant during the war.

Post Office industrial staff was added as follows: 1914—difference between total Post Office staff as given in "Report of the Postmaster General on the Post Office," 1913-1914, Cmd. 7573, 1914 (see also adjusted figures which exclude certain indirectly employed workers in *Statistical Abstract for the United Kingdom*, No. 82), and non-industrial staff as reported in Treasury return Cmd. 276, 1919. 1918—a figure derived from the average of the ratios of industrial to non-industrial staffs in 1914 and in 1920 as given in *Statistical Abstract for the United Kingdom*, No. 68.

Post Office, 1928: Data are from *Statistical Abstract for the United Kingdom*, No. 82. Other departments—numbers of industrial workers on April 1, 1929, as given in *Royal Commission on Civil Service, 1929*, Appendix I, "Introductory Memoranda Relating to the Civil Service," Treasury, H.M.S.O., 1930. These figures were referred to 1928.

1933: Letter from Treasury of January 29, 1954, to Mr. Alan T. Peacock, London School of Economics and Political Science.

1936, 1939, 1945, and 1950: See sources for non-industrial staffs in these years.

TABLE 4, *Parts B and C*

Based on Part A. In addition, in Part C:

TOTAL WORKING POPULATION

Figures shown in the table are ratios, the denominators of which are estimates of the working population. The estimates, except for 1939-1950, were obtained by straight-line interpolation between benchmark data derived from the Census and adjusted as indicated in notes to Table 1, above.

1914: Extrapolated from adjusted Census data for 1901 and 1911.

1918: Interpolated between adjusted Census data for 1911 and 1921; raised by 500,000 to take account of the wartime increase in the labor force that exceeded the war losses.

1928: Interpolated between adjusted Census data for 1921 and 1931.

1933: Extrapolated from adjusted Census data for 1921 and 1931.

1936: Interpolated between adjusted Census data for 1931 and the adjusted total for 1938 (see notes to Table 1, Total Working Population).

1939: Data are from H. Frankel, *op. cit.*

1945: Estimated by reference to "Distribution of Total Manpower, Great Britain," old series for June 1945 and old and new series for June 1948.

1950: Data are from "Distribution of Total Manpower, Great Britain," new series, for June 1950.

The absolute figures on which the percentages given in Table 4, Part C, are based are as follows:

1914	19,080,000	1936	22,219,000
1918	19,775,000	1939	22,916,000
1928	20,760,000	1945	24,237,000
1933	21,586,000	1950	23,068,000

TABLE 5

Based on Table 4, Part A.

TABLE 6

Based on Table 4, Part A. Data for 1955 are from Treasury Returns, "Staffs Employed in Government Departments," cited in *Annual Abstract of Statistics*, No. 92, 1955. The figure for the Armed Forces is from Ministry of Labour and National Service, "Distribution of Total Manpower, Great Britain," and refers to June 1954.

TABLE 7

Based on Table 4, Part A.

TABLE 8

CENSUS YEARS 1891-1931

Data are from Census of England and Wales and Census of Scotland.

1891 and 1901: *Occupation Tables*; 1911: *Occupation and Industry Tables*; 1921 and 1931: *Industry Tables*.

ADJUSTMENTS FOR 1891 AND 1901

Figures as given in source were raised by the estimated numbers of persons in the following services:

Utilities, 1891 and 1901: Figures shown in table are estimates arrived at as follows: The numbers of persons in gas, water, electricity, and tramway service—as reported in the *Occupation Tables* of the 1891 and 1901 Censuses —were raised by the ratio of the numbers in these industries, given in the *Occupation and Industry Tables* of the 1911 Census, to the corresponding numbers reported in the *Occupation Tables* of the 1911 Census. Then the ratios of local government workers to all workers attached to these industries were computed from the 1911 Census. The latter ratios were applied to the adjusted 1891 and 1901 Census data. The resulting figures were taken to represent the upper limit for local government workers in utilities.

Education, 1891: Figures shown in table are rough estimates, representing the number of teachers in Board Schools in England and Wales only. The estimate is based on the number of teachers in Board Schools in 1897, reported in C. A. Birchenough, *A History of Elementary Education in England and Wales from 1800 to the Present Day*, 1938, p. 334. In 1897 there were 59,760 teachers employed and paid by Local School Boards. Their number appears to have been considerably smaller at the beginning of the decade.

Education, 1901: The number of teachers in grant-aided schools in England and Wales as given in *The Report of the Ministry of Education for 1950*, "Education 1900-1950," p. 247, was 119,000. This figure was raised by the estimated number of teachers in grant-aided schools in Scotland and the estimated non-instructional staff in Great Britain. These estimates were derived by assuming that the ratio of persons in these two categories to the number of teachers in England and Wales, as given in the 1911 Census, was the same in 1901.

The figure shown in the table refers to the situation after the passing of the Balfour Education Act of 1902.

Others, 1891 and 1901: This category includes local administration (including Poor Law), sanitation, road maintenance, and miscellaneous services. The number of local government officials was given in the *Occupation Tables* of the Census—27,000 in 1891; 39,000 in 1901. The numbers in sanitary services and road maintenance were estimated by reference to the *Occupation Tables* of the 1891 and 1901 Censuses and the *Occupation and Industry Tables* of the 1911 Census (see above note on Utilities). The residual "Others" represents a rough estimate based on the ratio of local government officials—given in the *Occupation Tables* of the Census of England and Wales for 1911—to the number of non-specified local government workers reported in the *Industry Tables* of the same Census.

Figures shown in table under the heading "Others" are broken down as follows:

	1891	1901	1911
Municipal, parish, union, district officers, and other local and county officials	27,000	39,000	48,700
Poor Law			33,600
Sanitary services	5,000- 7,000	15,000-20,000	29,300
Road maintenance	10,000-15,000	20,000-35,000	37,300
Miscellaneous	15,000-25,000	30,000-45,000	99,300
Total	57,000-74,000	104,000-139,000	248,200

1938, 1945, AND 1948

Total local government employment (excluding fire service and civil defense) was estimated by reference to the following data:

a. The total number of persons in central and local government service, as shown in the source named below. This includes all non-industrial civil servants and those industrial central government workers who are not classified to a particular industry and all employees of local authorities (including teachers) other than those employed in trading services and, for 1945 and 1948, in the police force. Source: Ministry of Labour and National Service, "Distribution of Total Manpower," old series, cited in *Annual Abstract of Statistics*, No. 85, 1948.

b. The number of persons in the non-industrial civil service. Source: Treasury returns, cited in Annual Abstract of Statistics, No. 85, 1948 and No. 86, 1949.

c. The number of persons in the police force. Source: Home Office and Scottish Home Department, cited in *Annual Abstract of Statistics*, No. 85, 1948.

d. The number of persons in the trading services. Local government workers in this group were estimated by reference to data on total employment in gas, water, electricity tramway, and bus service, as reported in the *Ministry of Labour Gazette*; and by reference to the ratio of total employment to local government employment in these industries as given in the *Industry Tables* of the 1931 Census.

The figures shown in table were computed as follows:

	1938	1945	1948
Total number of persons in:			
Central and local government	1,386,000	1,903,000	2,128,000
Less: non-industrial civil service	363,000	705,000	693,000
Plus: police force	incl. in total	71,000	67,000
Plus: utilities	250,000	225,000	270,000
Total	1,237,000	1,494,000	1,772,000

(These estimates will be too high if a considerable number of industrial central government workers were not classified under a particular industry; they will be too low if industrial workers employed by local authorities—other than in public utilities—were classified under a particular industry and thus excluded from the totals for central and local government.)

1950

Data for total local government employment are from T. M. Ridley, *op.cit.*

EDUCATION, 1938, 1945, 1948, AND 1950

Data on numbers of teachers are from Ministry of Education for England and Wales and Education Department for Scotland, cited in *Annual Abstract of Statistics*, No. 88, 1952, and No. 90, 1953.

Adjustments: Figures for teachers as given in source were raised by 25 per cent to allow for non-instructional staffs whose number, as given in the Censuses rose from 11 per cent of the number of teachers in 1911 to 23 per cent in 1931. In view of the tendency of non-instructional staffs to rise relative to teachers, the allowance of 25 per cent may be insufficient, particularly in the more recent years. The 1946 data were referred to 1945.

1938 and 1945: Figures refer to full-time teachers and non-instructional staffs in grant-aided primary and secondary schools, including nursery, but excluding special, schools. The number of teachers in Scotland in 1945 was estimated on the basis of the ratio of teachers in England and Wales to teachers in Scotland in 1938 and 1948.

1950: Figure refers to full-time teachers and non-instructional staffs in all grant-aided schools, including special schools and establishments for further education. The number of teachers in Scotland, other than in primary and secondary schools, was estimated on the basis of the ratio of teachers in primary and secondary schools to teachers in special schools and establishments for further education in England and Wales.

POLICE, 1938, 1945, 1948 AND 1950:

Data are from Home Office and Scottish Home Department, cited in *Annual Abstract of Statistics*, No. 89, 1952.

Figures represent actual strength of the regular police force plus full-time auxiliaries; except for 1938, when data on full-time auxiliaries were not available.

TABLE 9

Coal mining: Data are from National Coal Board, *Reports and Accounts for 1950*. Figures represent annual average for industrial workers and refer to the end of 1949 for non-industrial employees.

Transportation: British Transport Commission, *Reports and Accounts for 1950*. Figures refer to the end of 1950.

Electricity supply: British Electricity Authority, *Reports and Accounts for March 1950–March 1951* and North of Scotland Hydro-Electric Board, *Reports and Accounts 1 January 1950–31 December 1951*. Figures refer to March 31, 1950.

Gas Supply: Gas Council, *Reports and Accounts for July 1948–March 1950*. Figures refer to March 31, 1950.

Civil aviation: British Overseas Airways Corporation, *Reports and Accounts for 1949-1950*. Figures refer to March 31, 1950. British European Airways Corporation, *Reports and Accounts for 1949-1950*. Figures refer to the beginning of the year.

British Broadcasting Corporation: *Annual Reports and Accounts of the British Broadcasting Corporation*, September 1950. Figures refer to March 31, 1950. Two part-time workers are counted as one full unit.

Regional board and teaching hospitals: *Report of the Ministry of Health for England and Wales for the Year Ending March 31, 1950* and *Reports of Department of Health for Scotland and the Scottish Health Service Council, 1953*, Cmd. 9107, H.M.S.O., Edinburgh. Figures for England and Wales refer to 1950, figures for Scotland refer to 1953. Two and one-half part-time workers are counted as one full unit.

Raw Cotton Commission: *Annual Report and Statement of Accounts for the Year Ending 31 July, 1950*.

TABLE 10

COMPARABILITY OF BRITISH AND UNITED STATES DATA

Most of the British data, especially those for the earlier period, are based on the Census. Most of the United States data (see Solomon Fabricant, *The Trend of Government Activity in the United States since 1900*, National Bureau of Economic Research, 1952) are drawn from the payrolls of federal government departments and local authorities. In this respect the American figures are probably more reliable than the British data, for payroll records are probably better than the reports of workers or their relatives. On the other hand, it was necessary for Fabricant to extrapolate the United States local government figures to years earlier than 1929 on the basis of a shrinking sample of state and city government payrolls, while even sample data for counties and minor civil divisions were utterly lacking. Fabricant was, however, able to confirm the broad character of his figures by comparison with data drawn from the early Censuses. What general inaccuracies stem from the unreliability of the sources, and what general biases are introduced into our comparison because of the difference in the character of our sources, we do not know; but some specific difficulties could be identified, and, to some extent, overcome.

The United States figures exclude unemployed workers throughout. The British figures do so from 1931 on, but not before. Unemployment in British government service, however, was very small before the Great Depression.

Our treatment of part-time workers was imposed upon us by the available data. The only figures available for Great Britain from 1900 to 1931 which cover all government were Census data. Except for errors these include all persons whose principal occupation was in a government job. (We might have used figures for central government from departmental sources in 1921 and 1931, but this change would have been of importance only for Civil Central Government, and local government employment would still have had to be based on Census information.) The figures, therefore, include those part-time workers the major portion of whose working time was in government but who nevertheless did not work full-time. These would presumably be few. After 1931 our British figures are derived from the payroll data of central government departments and from Ministry of Labour estimates based on incomplete payroll data of local authorities. We might have made allowances for part-time workers in central government in these years (as we do in Table 4, Parts A, B, and C, above), but it seemed better to carry the series through on a consistent basis since part-time work is not important in the late 1930's and 1940's.

Since the United States figures are based on payroll data, the original data include all part-time workers. Whether to allow for them or not, for purposes of the present comparison, is debatable. We should recall that the British Census data do make some allowance, for they exclude part-timers insofar as their government employment is minor and some other occupation is major, but they do not make full allowance. Our treatment of the United States figures is a compromise. We include the total number of government workers, both full- and part-time, in all categories but one, the Post Office, for reasons stated below.

We further justify our failure to allow for part-time work in the United States, outside the Post Office, by the following arguments: (1) There are no part-timers in the armed forces. (2) For the several departments of the federal government, other than the Post Office, Fabricant makes no allowance for part-time work and presumably part-timers were unimportant. (3) At the state and local level, part-timers were of some significance but they were not of major importance. In the public schools the full-time equivalent number of employees, as estimated by Fabricant, was 95 per cent of the total number in 1949 and 96 per cent in 1940. This latter percentage is constant in the figures since it was extrapolated from 1940 to 1900 by a sample of the total number. In non-school employment Fabricant estimates that the full-time equivalent number of workers was 85 per cent of the total in 1949 and 80 per cent in 1940. The latter figure again was extrapolated to earlier years. The use of Fabricant's figures without allowance for part-timers therefore does almost nothing to disturb the trend of his data in these categories. It serves to raise the level of state and local government employment about 15 per cent, and that of aggregate government

144

employment about 10 per cent, above the level that would result from reducing part-time work to its full-time equivalent. Reduction to the full-time equivalent number, however, would be too great for comparison with the British data, for, as already shown, the latter do include some part-timers. (4) We do, however, use Fabricant's full-time equivalent figures for the United States Post Office. The reason is that in this department part-time work was of dominant importance in the early decades of the century but declined markedly with the passage of years. Thus the full-time equivalent number was only 42 per cent of the total number of workers in 1900, but 90 per cent of the total in 1950. In view of the importance of the Post Office, the use of the total number would have greatly raised the level of the United States figures in the early years. It would have made federal employment 50 per cent larger than it now appears to have been in our table, and it would have underestimated its rate of growth. A clear picture of United States government employment, therefore, demands the use of full-time equivalent numbers in the Post Office. In this category, full-time equivalent numbers are also fairly comparable with the British data. For in the years 1911 to 1931 (1901 is an estimate) British Census data exclude most part-timers, and in 1938 and 1950, when our data include all part-timers (with the exception of sub-postmasters and sub-postmistresses in 1950), they are of minor significance. The full-time equivalent number was over 96 per cent of the total.

In the interval since our tables were prepared, the Department of Commerce has issued revised figures for public employment in education in the United States for years since 1940. The revisions reflect the incorporation of payroll and employment data collected by the Governments Division of the Census Bureau which the Department believes to be a more comprehensive count of employees than was previously issued by the Office of Education. This is stated to be especially true of non-teaching staffs, which include many part-time workers. The revised figures raise the estimated number of persons in public education by only a few thousand for 1940, but from 1,488,000 to 1,718,000 full- and part-time workers for 1950. The revised number of full-time equivalent workers in 1950 is estimated at 1,536,000.

We have not changed our tables to reflect these revisions because the new 1950 figure appears very large compared with the Census count for 1950, which was 1,539,000 including part-time workers whose main occupation was in public education. It should also be noted that if one accepts the revised figure for 1950, the ratio of teachers to total full- and part-time employees in public education falls to the implausibly low level of 0.594.

In considering the comparability of British and American figures for public education, it is necessary to remember that the size of the non-teaching staffs had to be estimated indirectly for Great Britain before 1911 and for the United States before 1929. For the years since 1931, the number of non-teaching employees in Great Britain has been estimated by reference to the ratio of non-teaching staffs as shown by the 1931 Census. A small allowance was made for the tendency of non-teaching staffs to grow in relative importance, but it is not clear whether we have made sufficient allowance.

SOURCES OF BRITISH DATA

National Defense
Armed forces: See Table 1.
Other defense: Figures represent non-industrial staffs of the service and

supply Departments as reported in the Treasury returns (see notes to Tables 3 and 4-A) plus industrial workers in government-owned establishments of a military character. The latter figures derived as follows:

1901: The estimated total number of industrial government workers was divided between defense and miscellaneous staffs by reference to Census figures for England and Wales for 1911. These showed some 85 per cent employed in establishments of a military character and some 15 per cent in others.

1911: Estimate based on the industrial classification of government workers as reported in the 1911 Census of England and Wales, *Occupation Tables*.

1921: Estimate based on the industrial classification of government workers as reported in the 1921 Census of England and Wales, *Industry Tables*. The total number of industrial workers in Scotland—reported in the 1921 Census of Scotland—was divided into defense and miscellaneous by reference to the corresponding proportions given in the 1931 Census of Scotland.

1931: Estimate based on the industrial classification of government workers as reported in the 1931 Census of England and Wales and Census of Scotland, *Industry Tables*.

1938 and 1950: Data are from Treasury returns "Industrial Staffs in the Civil Service," cited in *Annual Abstract of Statistics*, No. 85, 1948, and No. 89, 1952. Figures refer to workers employed by the Admiralty, the War Office, the Air Ministry, and in 1950, the Ministry of Supply.

Non-defense

Post Office, 1901: An estimate based on the Report of the Postmaster General of March 31, 1911, which lists 94,000 persons in the establishment of the Post Office, including sub-postmasters; and on "Return Showing the Total Number of Persons in the Established Civil Service of the State," Treasury Chambers, Cmd. 409, 1902, which reports 77,000 persons in the Post Office.

1911, 1921, and 1931: Census data.

1938 and 1950: Treasury returns "Staffs Employed in Government Departments."

Other, 1901: Census data plus government industrial workers (see notes to Table 1), less civilians engaged in National Defense, less Post Office.

1911, 1921, and 1931: Census data less civilians in National Defense, less Post Office.

1938 and 1950: Treasury data on non-industrial and industrial civil service staffs, less civilians engaged in National Defense, less Post Office.

State and Local Government

Data are from Table 8.

SOURCES OF UNITED STATES DATA

Figures shown in table are based on Solomon Fabricant, *The Trend of Government Activity in the United States since 1900*, National Bureau of Economic Research, 1952, Appendix B, Table B-14. This table covers the period 1900-1949. Data for 1950 were furnished by Robert E. Lipsey.

National Defense

Figures include armed forces, and employees in the War Department, Navy Department, and World War II agencies. See Fabricant, *op. cit.*, Appendix B, Table B-7.

Post Office

Figures represents full-time staffs. *Ibid.*, Appendix B, Table B-4.

Total Employment

1900-1940: *Ibid.*, Appendix B, Table B-1.

The 1950 figure is from *Census Release*, Series P-50, No 31, Annual Report on the Labor Force 1950; raised by 150,000 for omitted armed forces (see *Census Release* P-50, No. 2).

The absolute figures on which the percentages given in the table are based are as follows:

1900	26,984,000	1930	45,042,000
1910	35,649,000	1940	48,052,000
1920	40,212,000	1950	61,630,000

TABLE 11

POPULATION

Great Britain (including armed forces abroad), 1901, 1911, 1921, 1931: Census of England and Wales and Census and Scotland plus armed forces abroad (see notes to Table 1). 1939 and 1950: Registrars General mid-year estimates, cited in *Annual Abstract of Statistics*, No. 88.

United States, 1900-1950: Bureau of the Census population estimates for July 1 of each year, including armed forces abroad in 1930-1950, cited in *Statistical Abstract of the United States*, 1954.

GOVERNMENT EMPLOYEES

Ratios based on figures in Table 10.

TABLE 12

Based on Table 10.

TABLE 13

Data on total employment and Post Office employment in Great Britain and the United States are from Table 10.

American Telephone and Telegraph Workers: *Statistical Abstract of the United States*, 1930, pp. 359 and 364; 1943, pp. 412 and 419; 1954, pp. 525-526.

Figures for 1900, 1910, and 1920 actually refer to 1902, 1912, and 1922 respectively, dates when Census data on the communications industry were available. 1902 and 1930-1950 include ocean cable service. 1900 and 1910 cover telephone carriers with income over $5,000. 1930-1950 cover telephone carriers with income over $100,000.

TABLE 14

LINE

1. Figures are from Table 10.

2. Great Britain 1901: *Statistical Abstract of the United Kingdom*, No. 59, Tables 127, 143, and 145.

England and Wales 1950: Elementary and secondary schools from the *Report of the Ministry of Education for the Year 1950*, Cmd. 8244, 1951, Table 6. Includes 30,222 teachers in infant schools, of whom 2,010 taught classes of children entirely under five. Most others in infant schools taught classes "under 8, except entirely under 5."

Scotland 1950: Elementary and secondary schools from *Annual Abstract of Statistics*, No. 88, Table 96. Includes teachers in nursery, but not in special, schools.

Great Britain 1950, colleges and universities: Assumed to be the same as for all universities. From *Annual Abstract of Statistics*, No. 88, Table 121.

United States 1900 and 1950: Department of Health, Education, and Welfare, *Biennial Survey of Education*, 1948-1950, Chap. 1, Tables 7 and 13, and Chap. 4, Table 2. Of the total number of teachers in higher education in 1950, 22,900 were employed in teachers colleges, junior colleges, and normal schools not included in the British figures. Teachers in privately controlled universities and colleges in 1950 numbered 103,900, of whom 6,800 were in teachers colleges, etc.

3. Great Britain: Figures are from Table 1. The 1901 figure was reduced by the estimated number of unemployed. See Table 14, footnote c.

United States: Figures are from notes to Table 10.

4. Line 1 divided by line 3.

5. Line 2 divided by line 3.

6. Line 2 divided by line 1.

7. Great Britain: *Annual Abstract of Statistics*, No. 88, Tables 8 and 9. Age group 15-18 estimated at 80 per cent of age group 15-19. Age group 19-22 estimated at 20 per cent of age group 15-19 plus 60 per cent of age group 20-24.

United States: *Census of Population*, 1900, Vol. I, Part 2, and *Census of Population*, 1950, Vol. II, Part 1.

8. England and Wales, 1950: Age group 5-18 from Cmd. 8244, 1951, Table 2.

Scotland 1950: From *Annual Abstract of Statistics*, No. 88, Table 106. Includes grant-aided schools only.

Great Britain 1950: College and university students from *Annual Abstract of Statistics*, No. 88, Table 120. Includes universities only, enrollment of full- and part-time students for academic year 1949-1950.

United States: *Biennial Survey of Education*, 1948-1950. Age group 5-18 from Chap. 1, Tables 15 and 16. Age group 5-14 includes all children in kindergarten through 8th grade without regard to age. Age group 15-18 includes all children in grades 9-12 and high school postgraduates. College and university: *Ibid.*, Chap. 4, Table 1. Includes four-year colleges, junior colleges, technical and professional institutions offering work of college grade, universities, and institutions for education of teachers.

9. Great Britain 1901: *Statistical Abstract of the United Kingdom*, No. 59, Tables 127, 141, and 145. Age group 5-14 includes all students 5 years old and over enrolled in elementary and higher elementary schools. There were no regular government-maintained secondary schools in England in 1901. Information on secondary schools in England and Wales is not available until 1905, when there were 94,698 pupils.

Great Britain 1950: *See* sources for line 8.

United States: *Biennial Survey of Education*, 1948-1950. Age group 5-18 from Chap. 1, Table 13. College and university from Chap. 4, Table 2.

10. Line 7 divided by line 3.

11. Line 9 divided by line 8.

12. Line 9 divided by line 7.

13. Line 2 divided by line 9.

14. Line 3 divided by total population (see Table 11).

15. Line 3 divided by total population minus population 18 and under (see sources for line 7).

TABLE 15

Based on Table 10.

INDEX OF PERSONS AND
GOVERNMENT AGENCIES

RECENT AND FORTHCOMING
PUBLICATIONS OF THE
NATIONAL BUREAU OF ECONOMIC RESEARCH

NATIONAL BUREAU BOOKS *are available from bookstores or Princeton University Press, Princeton, New Jersey, except that contributors and subscribers to the National Bureau should order directly from the Bureau.* OCCASIONAL PAPERS, TECHNICAL PAPERS, *and* ANNUAL REPORTS *are available from the National Bureau of Economic Research, 261 Madison Avenue, New York 16, New York.*

BOOKS

The Growth of Public Employment in Great Britain (1956)	166 pp.	$3.75
Moses Abramovitz and Vera Eliasberg		
The Pattern of Financial Asset Ownership:		
Wisconsin Individuals, 1949 (1956)	196 pp.	3.75
Thomas R. Atkinson		
Personal Income during Business Cycles (1956)	208 pp.	4.00
Daniel Creamer		
Consumption and Business Fluctuations: A Case Study of the		
Shoe, Leather, Hide Sequence (1956) 8½ x 11	320 pp.	7.50
Ruth P. Mack		
Urban Mortgage Lending: Comparative Markets		
and Experience (1956)	212 pp.	4.00
J. E. Morton		
Trends in Employment in the Service Industries (1956)	187 pp.	3.75
George J. Stigler		
Problems of Capital Formation: Concepts, Measurement,		
and Controlling Factors (1956) (planographed)	618 pp.	7.50
Studies in Income and Wealth, Volume Nineteen		
Policies to Combat Depression (1956)	428 pp.	8.50
Special Conference Series No. 7		
Distribution's Place in the American Economy		
since 1869 (1955)	240 pp.	4.50
Harold Barger		
Minimum Price Fixing in the Bituminous Coal Industry		
(1955)	554 pp.	10.00
Waldo E. Fisher and Charles M. James		
Input-Output Analysis: An Appraisal (1955)	383 pp.	7.50
Studies in Income and Wealth, Volume Eighteen		
Short-Term Economic Forecasting (1955)	520 pp.	7.50
Studies in Income and Wealth, Volume Seventeen		
Capital Formation and Economic Growth (1955)	691 pp.	12.00
Special Conference Series No. 6		
Business Concentration and Price Policy (1955)	524 pp.	9.00
Special Conference Series No. 5		
The Frontiers of Economic Knowledge (1954)	376 pp.	5.00
Arthur F. Burns		
Mortgage Lending Experience in Agriculture (1954)	257 pp.	5.00
Lawrence A. Jones and David Durand		
Long-Range Economic Projection (1954)	488 pp.	9.00
Studies in Income and Wealth, Volume Sixteen		
Regularization of Business Investment (1954)	539 pp.	8.00
Special Conference Series No. 4		
The Volume of Corporate Bond Financing since 1900 (1953)	464 pp.	7.50
W. Braddock Hickman		

Shares of Upper Income Groups in Income and Savings
(1953)   768 pp. $9.00
   Simon Kuznets
The Trend of Government Activity in the United States since
1900 (1952)   288 pp.   4.00
   Solomon Fabricant

OCCASIONAL PAPERS

53. *Productivity Trends: Capital and Labor* (1956) $0.50
   John W. Kendrick
52. *Resource and Output Trends in the United States*
since 1870 (1956)   0.50
   Moses Abramovitz
51. *Interest as a Source of Personal Income and Tax Revenue* (1956)   1.25
   Lawrence H. Seltzer
50. *Agricultural Equipment Financing* (1955)   1.25
   Howard G. Diesslin
49. *The Korean War and United States Economic Activity,*
1950-1952 (1955)   0.75
   Bert G. Hickman
48. *A Century and a Half of Federal Expenditures* (1955)   1.25
   M. Slade Kendrick
47. *The Ownership of Tax-Exempt Securities, 1913-1953* (1955)   1.50
   George E. Lent
46. *Immigration and the Foreign Born* (1954)   1.50
   Simon Kuznets and Ernest Rubin
45. *Capital and Output Trends in Mining Industries, 1870-1948*
(1954)   1.00
   Israel Borenstein
44. *The Growth of Physical Capital in Agriculture, 1870-1950* (1954) 1.25
   Alvin S. Tostlebe
43. *Trends and Cycles in Capital Formation by United States Railroads,*
1870-1950 (1954)   1.50
   Melville J. Ulmer
42. *The Share of Financial Intermediaries in National Wealth and*
National Assets, 1900-1949 (1954)   1.50
   Raymond W. Goldsmith

TECHNICAL PAPERS

11. *Fiscal-Year Reporting for Corporate Income Tax* (1956)   1.25
   W. L. Crum
10. *Factors Influencing Consumption: An Experimental*
Analysis of Shoe Buying (1954)   2.00
   Ruth P. Mack
 9. *The Volume of Residential Construction, 1889-1950* (1954)   1.50
   David M. Blank

ANNUAL REPORTS (GRATIS)

By Solomon Fabricant
36th. *Basic Research and the Analysis of Current Business Conditions*
   (May 1956)
35th. *Government in Economic Life* (May 1955)
34th. *Economic Progress and Economic Change* (May 1954)